T0152517

UNSEEN

It is truly comforting to hear from someone that has the same struggles and experiences as you. This book has the potential to help veterans recover and help others understand why the recovery process is so fragile, yet tedious. This book gives an unusually authentic insight into the daily issues and psyche of the combat vet."

—**Samantha Snead**, Air Force veteran

"Honest, real, sincere should be standard issue for anyone working with veterans and service members alike. The chapters spoke to me in ways that summed up things I had felt through service and working with veterans after. I couldn't have defined it any better. Elisa has the standard operating procedure for anyone who works with and cares for those who have served."

—**Mariel Juarez**, LCSW, readjustment counselor,
Army Iraq veteran

"I was moved by reading and felt less shameful about my own experience in the military as I read 'Being uncomfortable and embarrassed about feelings might lead to suffering all alone. Suffering all alone means being the judge and jury of everything we do. That is emotionally hazardous, especially if we already hate ourselves for something as simple as being human.' As I continued to read, I was able to reflect and then let go of some of the trauma that happened while I served. I was able to develop some insight into how I process through others' narratives and still imagine myself through their struggles. *Unseen* is both informative and healing in talking about our shame and courage in being in."

—**Alveen "Bre" Bregaudit**, LMSW,
U.S. Army Afghanistan veteran

UNSEEN

Uncovering the Invisible Wounds
of Military Trauma

ELISA ESCALANTE

AITIA PRESS • NEW YORK

UNSEEN

Uncovering the Invisible Wounds of Military Trauma

© 2021 **ELISA ESCALANTE**

Published in New York, New York, by Aitia Press, a branded imprint of Morgan James Publishing. Morgan James is a trademark of Morgan James, LLC. www.morganjamespublishing.com

ISBN 978-1-63195-353-8 paperback
ISBN 978-1-63195-354-5 eBook
Library of Congress Control Number: 2020919978

Cover Design by:
Rachel Lopez
www.r2cdesign.com

Morgan James is a proud partner of Habitat for Humanity Peninsula and Greater Williamsburg. Partners in building since 2006.

Get involved today! Visit
www.MorganJamesBuilds.com

To Bethany, for encouraging me to finish this book and seeing its potential. To my mother, Ruby, for teaching me about suffering. To my grandmother, Belia, for teaching me kindness. To my father, Edward, a twenty-year Marine veteran, for giving me confidence. To my stepmother, Mary, for teaching me perseverance. To my brothers, Anthony, Kody, Brock, and Nathan, for being my sidekicks. To my best friend, Rebeca, for giving me hope. To my love, John, for teaching me about self-acceptance.

And to my fellow veterans for your service, dedication, courage, and strength. I'm happy that I have you with me in this life.

TABLE OF CONTENTS

"At the end of the day, I am left wanting to unlearn what I have learned. I want to push out the new, that is now permanently tangled within my mind. I am left with new scars every day."

Introduction

IT'S NOT WHAT YOU
SEE IN THE MOVIES

"Acknowledge that I am fighting a battle you cannot understand; you are fighting one I cannot understand. And instead of debating over who has it worse, we support each other through it all. We are all fighting against something."

◇◇

Trigger Warning!
There are verbatim quotations—trauma stories—throughout this book that are clearly distinguished from the

surrounding text if you wish to pause and prepare before reading.

❖-❖

I refused to watch another war film after I got back home from Afghanistan.

It wasn't the triggering factor for me as much as it was an issue I had with how post-traumatic stress disorder (PTSD) was being portrayed to the general public. When I told a few family members that I didn't want to see war movies, they convinced me to watch just one more. They promised I would love it...but I hated it—another cliché portrayal of war trauma.

Often, the reason the movies get it wrong is because you cannot merely be shown trauma on screen and understand it. Someone cannot simply explain what they have experienced to you; you must experience it yourself. If you do not feel it, you do not know it. This concept applies to all mental illnesses, including PTSD, and it is why the stigma surrounding mental illness exists in the first place. Outside of the human mind, it is truly unknown and unseen.

In the clinical world, we now use the term "invisible wounds" to explain mental illnesses, and, with that in mind, there are two phrases I personally forbid myself from saying in all clinical therapy sessions:

1. "I understand" (Even if you do understand, they do not need to know that.)
2. "It will all be okay" (Seriously, how can anyone make this promise?)

I avoid those phrases in all my sessions with the intention of making sure my client knows that I am not trying to mislead them—my knowledge only goes so far. I must listen to them to know what is happening, but chances are, I may not be able to relate completely. Our nice, beautiful, well-written manual of mental health disorders (currently known as the DSM-V) merely contains guidelines. It is not a tell-all. A therapist is not meant to know what someone has gone through. A therapist is trained to treat people for illnesses and stressors, but therapists are not mind readers. If they are truthful with themselves and their clients, they will not pretend to know all the answers.

Neither therapists nor films can capture and understand the full extent of someone's suffering. We are not capable of experiencing how another person suffers. We can be sad that another person is suffering—we can even be empathetic—and we can suffer in our own way having knowledge of it, but I cannot feel how someone suffers, as they cannot feel how I suffer.

Movies are meant to put money into the pockets of the people who created it. And to fulfill that purpose, a movie must appeal to the audience. An audience wants action, drama, comedic relief, or those butterfly feelings when something meaningful happens. An audience does not want to see someone chronically suffering, day in and day out, during tedious, average, boring days. The audience wants to see the glamour and action of war, not the down days when troops are bored out of their minds.

When you watch war or portrayal of PTSD in a film, you do not get the raw experience of war, and you do not know PTSD. I don't write that with any hate or pessimism but with the intentions of education and information. Please do not tell your loved one who just got back from war that you understand what they went through because you watched the most recent war movie. And definitely do not try to convince them that they should watch it too.

Sometimes I have veteran clients who do want to watch war movies because they consider it to be a good part of their healing process, or a way to get more trigger exposure in a safe environment. However, what more commonly presents are veterans triggered by the news, war movies, or war documentaries. Simply put, they're angry when watching these things because it is nothing like what they actually experienced. It feels like an insult, discrediting what they went through during war. For a veteran, it isn't a movie; it was real life. And the end result in real life when it comes to war experiences is rarely a happy one, or a love story, or a story of valor and pride. As you'll read, the end result is more often a story of confusion, tragedy, trauma, grief, and suffering.

This book is not an extensive study of PTSD nor does it cover even half of the obstacles veterans face throughout the course of their military career or adjustment period post-service. It is meant to be an empathetic resource—a way forward—for veterans, their loved ones, and anyone else who interacts with those who have served on a regular basis. One of my goals is to help mitigate the cultural gap between veterans and civilians, as well as help with the ongoing efforts to decrease military and veteran rates of suicide. I hope it serves you well and sheds some light on the realities veterans with PTSD and moral injuries face every day, both in war and returning home.

PART I

THERAPY

THERAPY IN A WAR ZONE

"When you are forced to find peace in chaos and suffering, you will be chaotic even in peace. You can take the human out of the nightmare, but the nightmare is still in them."

I spent my junior and senior year of undergrad, as well as my year in grad school, focusing mainly on military issues and veteran affairs. It only made sense since I spent six years as an active duty Air Force mental health technician before I got out of the military and transferred to the Silver School of Social Work at NYU.

One project during those focused studies felt very special to me, and it wasn't because it was my best work. It was the title I chose for the presentation. Quite honestly, I don't even remember what I presented on, but the title still intrigues me: "Therapy in a War Zone."

I repeat that phrase in my head quite often, and I think about how contradictory it sounds. To give therapy in a hazardous environment. Is that even possible? The Department of Defense (DOD) initiated many mental health programs, alcohol and substance abuse services, and family advocacy departments. Both Operation Iraqi Freedom and Operation Enduring Freedom created a high need for increased mental health services, to include sending mental health teams to war zones. This was the very reason I deployed to Afghanistan in 2012 to an Army FOB (forward operating base) in Jalalabad working with a combat stress team of six. Our main responsibilities included helping soldiers cope mentally and emotionally with the many stressors that come with living in a war zone and engaging in combat.

⟡⟡⟡⟡⟡⟡⟡⟡⟡⟡⟡⟡⟡⟡⟡⟡⟡⟡⟡⟡⟡⟡⟡⟡⟡⟡⟡⟡⟡⟡⟡⟡⟡⟡⟡

"We were going through one of our most intense battles. Out of seventy-five people, only fifteen of us survived. I remember looking over at my friend, not being able to recognize what I was seeing. His entire top half was blown off. I saw his ribs, nothing else above that was left. He had only four days left in the deployment when he was killed. I didn't think I would make it home after that."

⟡⟡⟡⟡⟡⟡⟡⟡⟡⟡⟡⟡⟡⟡⟡⟡⟡⟡⟡⟡⟡⟡⟡⟡⟡⟡⟡⟡⟡⟡⟡⟡⟡⟡⟡

There is something very unique about military mental health: We're expected to somehow heal people just enough so that we can keep them in danger longer. It feels like putting band-aids on stab wounds, quite honestly, and it hurt me to do so. My major ethical dilemma consisted of constantly being torn between my roles as a mental health worker and a military member. I had a mission, yes, but I had a code of ethics as well. And the lines blurred at times. Many of my colleagues felt this way as well.

The other piece that makes military mental health unique is that we, mental health workers, are deployed to the war zones with our clients, possibly confronted with danger ourselves. We would hear trauma stories from our clients about attacks we were exposed to. Talk about countertransference! Can we help people heal if they remain in the same dangerous environment, or are we there to convince them that they are "okay" enough to stay? Some clients would even ask me who I go to if I need any counseling resources.

I still don't know the answer to that one. If I were to try and get therapy from the therapists I worked alongside, that would have been a major conflict of interest. For everyone's sake, most medics and mental health workers pretend to be "okay" while they are in war zones because they need to tend to their mission of healing the warriors.

◊◊◊◊◊◊◊◊◊◊◊◊◊◊◊◊◊◊◊◊◊◊◊◊◊◊◊◊◊◊◊◊◊◊

"We were patrolling on foot and all of a sudden there was a pop right next to my coworker's foot and hot sand hit my face. My initial thought was that I may have had an accidental discharge. But shortly after, I realized my friend had stepped on a landmine right next to me. His entire lower leg was blown off. I pulled him away from the hot zone."

◦◦◦◦◦◦◦◦◦◦◦◦◦◦◦◦◦◦◦◦◦◦◦◦◦◦◦◦◦◦◦◦◦◦◦◦◦

The constant pressure from our higher-ups and the mission reinforced everything about this chaotic and conflicting work environment, almost making it feel "normal." It was my normal. It was literally what I had trained for, and I truly wanted to save everyone I could from the emotional impact of war zone trauma. I also tried my best to empathize with and acknowledge that military leadership also had some ethical dilemmas they faced on the daily: being mission-oriented for war demands versus being people-oriented. Being people-oriented required learning that these warriors, regardless of how amazingly trained they are, are human and have emotional and mental needs.

So, which one would it be?

"Hey! This pilot is drinking alcohol. We want to keep this between us. Can you guys just make sure he's not an alcoholic? We need to get him flying again ASAP!"

"Hey! Our guy was caught huffing canned air again. Will you just talk to him for a while? We gotta get him back to working on the engines. We don't understand why he keeps doing this."

"Hey! This soldier shot and killed himself! What did you guys miss? What did you say to him? Why couldn't you see this coming?"

(Then comes the investigation.)

◦◦

"I was in a lot of fire fights. I was shot at, saw my friends get shot, some of them killed. There were RPGs flying over my head as well as mortars. There was one that hit so close to me that all I saw was white, and all I heard was ringing. I wasn't sure if I was dead or alive anymore."

◦◦

We were the ones they could place all responsibility on when they feared blaming themselves: the combat stress team. It no longer had to be the fault of the commander, or the first sergeant, or the direct supervisor, the hostile work environment, the peers, the family back home harassing them for more money, the cheating spouse, the lack of coping mechanisms, or the constant exposure to near-death experiences with limited time off. Now there is an opportunity to send soldiers to get "healed" and ready for battle once again—or to blame their "failure" or suicide on the combat stress team. Because, due to the many reasons listed above, among others, we cannot always provide foolproof "Therapy in a War Zone." The first step of healing is establishing safety, and we are not safe in war—period.

I must say though, despite all the challenges, "Therapy in a war zone" helps many deployed military members, even with all the external factors working against us. While deployed, I learned to be in the moment with clients and work to instill just a sliver of hope that one day the nightmare will all be over—if we could make it home of course.

THE PRESENTATION: SLEEPY OR ANGRY

"Sometimes, getting answers is the answer. Connecting truth with a reason why. We deserve to know why we suffer, even if the cure is unknown."

When a veteran with PTSD walks into the doors of a mental health facility, they typically present with one of two things: anger problems or sleep disturbance.

They present with these two issues most often because they're safe topics to talk about. Anger is a safe and acceptable emotion for the time being. It has very little stigma attached to it compared with other emotions. It's also a very understandable emotion that society will accept from a person who just came home from a war zone, assuming there are no serious behavioral issues attached to it.

And sleep? Well, we evidently need sleep to survive. If anyone has trouble sleeping, it's very understandable to seek treatment for it.

⬦⬦⬦⬦⬦⬦⬦⬦⬦⬦⬦⬦⬦⬦⬦⬦⬦⬦⬦⬦⬦⬦⬦⬦⬦⬦⬦⬦⬦⬦⬦⬦⬦

"I was walking with my platoon through the jungle. All of a sudden an explosion went off right beside us. I still don't know what exactly it was. But it blew off half of the guy's head right in front of me. His brains were all over my face."

⬦⬦⬦⬦⬦⬦⬦⬦⬦⬦⬦⬦⬦⬦⬦⬦⬦⬦⬦⬦⬦⬦⬦⬦⬦⬦⬦⬦⬦⬦⬦⬦⬦

But all other symptoms and emotions related to trauma remain unspoken and forbidden: sadness, grief, guilt, shame, intrusive thoughts, nightmares, hypervigilance, flashbacks, isolation, etc. These emotions, symptoms, and defense mechanisms, especially for male veterans, are seen as a weakness. They are seen as getting in the way of the task at hand, and, truth be told, they could be very hazardous in a life or death situation. Training people for war means training them to shut down any fear or hesitation in order to accomplish dangerous missions. Thus, feelings and fear can no longer be a part of the equation, even when no longer in a war zone.

⬦⬦⬦⬦⬦⬦⬦⬦⬦⬦⬦⬦⬦⬦⬦⬦⬦⬦⬦⬦⬦⬦⬦⬦⬦⬦⬦⬦⬦⬦⬦⬦⬦

"When I got to my unit, they didn't have any rooms in the barracks available yet. The unit had to decide where I would stay. They snickered as they picked the sergeant I would be rooming with for the night. I didn't understand why until later. That night he forced himself onto me. I was ashamed and didn't want to report. No one back then would believe a man could get sexually assaulted anyways. I had to work with him an entire year after that happened. He would talk to me and ask me how I was, and if I was okay. As if nothing happened at all."

❖❖❖❖❖❖❖❖❖❖❖❖❖❖❖❖❖❖❖❖❖❖❖❖❖❖❖❖❖❖

The other important factor in how PTSD presents is that the main defense mechanisms used to protect against trauma are avoidance and isolation. People avoid thinking about what happened and avoid being reminded by running from external stimuli that could trigger their memories, sometimes even going to the extreme of avoiding going outside their homes. Things like noises, crowds, and smells have the potential to be triggers. To avoid thinking about trauma, they suppress their thoughts and emotions. They push memories away through obsessive work schedules or compulsive behaviors, including substance abuse. They may also dive into helping others and put themselves last. It's easier to deal with other people's issues than to confront your own.

With all of this being said, therapists have a huge challenge sitting across from them in the therapy chair. The big question is: "How do I get this veteran to tell me that they have been traumatized, knowing that they will most likely be triggered by just speaking about it and that speaking about it is forbidden in their world?"

I can't stress enough that this is, in large part, the clinician's responsibility. It is the therapist's job to not only see any red flags, but also to know what to ask and how to ask it. Many therapists go into trauma work learning that building trust with the client is essential, and the intricacy of how we word our questions is crucial.

Plenty of veterans blame themselves for being misdiagnosed. They report that they failed by not sharing enough with previous therapists, that they held back information or minimized their own experiences. I always assure those veterans that it is not their fault. All of those avoidance behaviors are to be expected from a veteran who suffers from PTSD. If the traumatized veteran saw a clinician, yet their PTSD was not diagnosed, it typically means one or both of two things:

1. The clinician did not gain their trust.
2. The clinician did not ask the right questions.

Yes, it would be much easier if clients could just tell the whole truth, and nothing but the truth, but through military training and experiences, they learn to filter and become hardened human beings who can no longer identify or express emotions. There's a wall between the veteran and everyone else around them—including the therapist.

One of the most common lines I hear from traumatized clients in general has to do with just "leaving the past in the past" where it belongs. Many still cling to the myth that the past cannot harm us because it is gone, but, on the contrary, memory has everything to do with how we act and how we react to everything in the present. How can a traumatized person leave the past when it is directly impacting their physiological, cognitive, and emotional responses on a daily basis?

Many veterans with PTSD show evidence of significant effort spent trying to suppress their memories and emotional pain. This is where the suffering starts, as it is unnatural to continue trying to force your brain to forget about what it is not done processing.

One veteran client expressed, "Happy or angry, happy and angry! That is it! That is all I ever feel!" Those two emotions were all he had the ability to feel when he first presented for treatment. Due to war trauma, he had adapted into a human being who numbed and blocked the majority of his emotions, leaving him unable to connect emotionally, causing strain in his marriage. Want to guess what his initial presentation and chief complaints were though? Angry and unable to sleep.

FUNCTIONING, BUT NOT FINE

"Remember, we are not necessarily seeing the worst of the worst. We are seeing the ones that are willing to reach out for help. Everyone else remains hidden."

My very first commander (a psychologist) used to say, "The most dangerous person is the one in the waiting room that we have not yet assessed."

There is a dangerous myth society clings to, and, sadly, some mental health professionals cling to as well: If a person is functioning in their daily life and does not seem to be impaired in any way (i.e., stable job, good income, family life looks fine, smiles, socializes) then, surely, they are fine. I've seen the shock

15

again and again from people who cling to this myth, as the people who are "fine" kill themselves at alarming rates.

Sometimes these suicides came from people who were never hospitalized, never sought help, who always seemed "okay" and never spoke up.

And that is the problem. Read that last sentence again!

We can all pretend to be okay. As a matter of fact, humans are actors every day in that sense. What would happen if the world could always see how we feel? What a vulnerable and scary world that would be. Not to mention the fact that, in many cases, when people take the risk of "venting" or divulging any information regarding their emotional pain, there's a chance it will just get met with criticism and judgement.

So, "functioning" by society's standards does not mean fine. It is not about what a person can force themselves to do; it is about what it costs them to do it. How hard is it for them to get out of bed every day? To work a full-time job with debilitating symptoms? Keep up with constantly suppressing emotions? Hiding struggles to avoid "burdening" other people?

There is no population more talented and trained at being high-functioning while mentally ill than military members and veterans. These are groups trained to be high-functioning while being put through misery and debilitating mental and physical stressors. Pain is seen as weakness—emotions as weakness—and taking breaks is forbidden. Not completing the mission means you've failed. Easing your pain and taking a load off can equal death for a fellow military member. Mistakes are unacceptable. Mistakes are for humans, and you can't be a needy human when there is war.

◦◦◦◦◦◦◦◦◦◦◦◦◦◦◦◦◦◦◦◦◦◦◦◦◦◦◦◦◦◦◦◦◦◦◦

"They shot at our truck and tried to mortar us too. The vehicle flipped over and over and I was a medic just trying to make sure the men were strapped in and okay, along with keeping myself secure. One of the bullets just grazed by my eye and gave me vision problems for the rest of my life, along with that vehicle accident causing me chronic pain throughout the right side of my body forever."

◦◦◦◦◦◦◦◦◦◦◦◦◦◦◦◦◦◦◦◦◦◦◦◦◦◦◦◦◦◦◦◦◦◦◦

Veterans will rarely cry out for help. Their behaviors will tell you more than their words ever will. And, often, the behaviors are so terrifying or difficult to deal with that it's easier to label them as a "crazy vet" than to actually see the reality that this is a person who is in a tremendous amount of pain and has no idea how to express that pain—or how to start healing. If there is erratic behavior, it is often not coincidence but rather traumatic grief and moral injury met with burnout.

In fact, veterans are so experienced and crafty when it comes to hiding their pain and functioning at all costs, even professionals have a hard time picking up on their pain. Veterans can trick us into thinking they are "fine" long before they are actually fine. They have adapted the mentality that they are "wrong" if they are tired, stressed, unhappy, or emotional. The mentality says, "Suck it up, because we are all in this together, and we are all fine."

This is a population of people who require a lot of training, experience, time, patience, and care to help. They might self-sabotage when they're about to receive help. They might get defensive or angry as their emotions come to the surface. Or they might just run away the moment you get somewhere. Being an emotional being feels too vulnerable and risky. Many veterans do not believe they have the time for self-expression. They're already thinking about the next mission after the military: school, a job, family, caregiving, fitness, etc. They often jump right into the new mission post-service so that many of their friends and family members see them as fine or "high speed."

❖❖❖❖❖❖❖❖❖❖❖❖❖❖❖❖❖❖❖❖❖❖❖❖❖❖❖❖❖❖❖❖❖

"We had this one crazy sergeant who was losing his mind. There were dead enemies all around us that we didn't clean up yet. Every morning he would shoot them in the head again. All of them, while saying, 'Die mother f***er! Die mother f***er!' He just kept on shooting new bullets in their heads."

❖❖❖❖❖❖❖❖❖❖❖❖❖❖❖❖❖❖❖❖❖❖❖❖❖❖❖❖❖❖❖❖❖

That is why I do not believe in "firing" clients for non-compliance. Patience and a respect for freedom of choice and will is a necessity when it comes to serving veterans. It takes a good amount of time to break through the walls of people who have been trained to develop a hardened wall of defenses. It is not uncommon for a veteran to run away after one or two sessions, never to be heard from again. It is also common for those same veterans to come back one day, sometimes over a year later! It often takes long-term therapy to get somewhere, and, unfortunately, what we have on the market for PTSD treatment is usually very short-term therapy.

Overall, veterans are convinced they are perfectly fine—as long as they can function enough to complete the mission. There is no more self-care, just sacrifice. If you are living and breathing, you are fine. The mission and the leadership need their teams to be fine so badly that they do everything in their power to make everyone fine. Punished until they get it right, veterans have their minds cemented in a doctrine that requires them to be as close to perfect as they possibly can be; perfectly functioning is the only acceptable way to be for war.

But, unfortunately, many of them are not fine as they portray themselves to be.

YOU ARE NOT TO BE TRUSTED

"I truly believe we can destroy ourselves internally, before anyone else can even get a chance."

I mention the importance of trust many times; yet, we are not to be trusted. Many veterans believe mental health professionals cannot be trusted, for reasons like: "Well because according to friends and leadership, going to mental health means I can lose my security clearance or top secret clearance." "It means I may not be deployable for overseas assignments." "It means I might get med boarded and removed from the military altogether!"

Or the conversation might go something like:

"Okay, so, perhaps talk to your leadership about your stress instead?"

"If I talk to leadership about what's going on, they might punish me or see me as weak." "I saw a coworker tell his supervisor he was struggling and next thing I know they command directed him to go to mental health...then the next thing I know he vanishes and never comes back!"

Okay, so, talk to your battle buddy?

"My battle buddy has enough on his hands. He's going through worse. I don't want to burden them with my issues." "Last time I confided in a peer, they gave me horrible advice. It didn't really help."

Okay, so, talk to your spouse or family?

"They wouldn't understand! They're civilians!" "How does talking about it help the issue? No one is going to do anything for me anyways." "I can handle this on my own."

◊◦◊◦◊◦◊◦◊◦◊◦◊◦◊◦◊◦◊◦◊◦◊◦◊◦◊◦◊◦◊◦◊◦◦◦◦

"It was their hazing ritual on the ship. 'This is a test we put everyone through,' they would say. They taped some of us to the pipes, equipment, or weapons, said we were being tape tested. And proceeded to mess with our genitals. The more painful it was, the more they were testing our ability to endure pain. I was supposed to be as silent as possible during the pain."

◊◦◊◦◊◦◊◦◊◦◊◦◊◦◊◦◊◦◊◦◊◦◊◦◊◦◊◦◊◦◊◦◊◦◦◦◦

I have heard the phrase "I can handle it on my own" so many times that I almost want to make it the military motto.

I've heard that phrase sometimes years after clients have started therapy. They feel like they have to handle it all on their own because the obstacles to getting help are very real.

In a world where you are owned by a contract and must serve your time, options are limited and people aren't to be trusted. The one good thing is that mental health services are free for military members and many veterans. But that doesn't do them much good if they avoid using those services because they have lost all trust and hope in the government that may have burned them a few times too many.

Then there's the question of who really has the veterans' best interests at heart. The military needs them to perform. Their dependents need them to work and provide. The mental health clinic might make recommendations that could be career changers—or enders. Their outside family assumes they are taken care of because they have money and a roof over their head, and, supposedly, that is everything you need.

⊙-⊙

"For some reason, the officer in charge of us forced us to stop on the highway just to look around at the dead bodies. This was only a couple of weeks after the fatal incident. We saw the rotting bodies and broken-down vehicles for miles and miles."

⊙-⊙

The reality is, most military members who receive counseling get to stay in the military, but it's a risk many are not willing to take. Their job is their life, and they cannot afford to lose it. I have stressed many times during reintegration briefings when military members return from a war zone that voluntarily getting help is far better than getting into trouble due to behavioral issues stemming from mental health problems. I always encourage them to be proactive, but the fear and stigma runs deep, regardless of outreach efforts.

The transition to civilian life inevitably happens with or without counseling. But often without counseling, the military member turns into a veteran who cannot trust. And then when applying for veterans' benefits, they get an endless series of referrals and the dreaded runaround for months on end. Military members are conditioned to expect a system that does things efficiently and effectively. In their eyes, the civilian workforce is far from that. The Department of Veterans Affairs (VA), which is mainly comprised of civilians, does not move at a pace that veterans are accustomed to. There are many who give up. And the VA providers and case managers are added to their list of people who cannot be trusted.

"They sent me to this person who sent me to this person who sent me to this person and no one helped." "They never returned my calls." "They do not care."

Sometimes this is about miscommunication; sometimes the veteran is guarded and will not share how emergent their situation really is. Or, sometimes, the workers are either understaffed, incompetent, poorly trained, or burned out.

The fact is, you're damned if you do choose to trust someone and damned if you don't. If a veteran finally comes to terms with and acknowledges the military caused mental health issues and applies for disability without ever seeking counseling, there's a lack of evidence, and their case isn't as strong. The Veterans Benefits Administration does not know a person's individual story; all they have to go off of is the evidence put in front of them. It is hard to build this evidence in an organization that shames and often punishes mental health issues.

When a veteran is constantly rejected and pushed away from services they felt they were promised once upon a time, rage builds up. Rejection invalidates a person's experiences and traumas.

"I have no one to trust, no one who believes me, and no one who wants to help. I'm on my own."

That anger and rage aren't just about what happened to people while they were serving. That rage is about what happens when they are done. How well are they being taken care of following physical and emotional injuries from fighting wars for their country? Is there anyone they can trust?

SPECIFICITY

"No one is entitled to hear another person's truth, a person telling you their truth is always an unearned privilege."

Do not, I repeat, do not underestimate the power of specific questions—especially with the military and veteran populations.

If I were to ask a combat veteran, "Have you experienced anything traumatic?" there is a pretty good chance they will say "no" even if they experienced serious traumas. Again, one factor may be avoidance or the stigma and shame that come with trauma. But another important factor is that they have seen or heard of too many people who "had it worse."

"Well, that guy died so…I got lucky." "That person got their leg blown off…so…nothing like that happened to me." "The country I deployed to didn't have running water and their people lived in shacks, so we're (Americans) all lucky!"

So you have to get specific. My go-to questions typically include:

- "What was the worst part of your deployment experience?"
- "What stressed you out?"
- "Was there ever a time you feared for your life?"
- "Have you ever experienced the following symptoms?"

I re-evaluate this list with each client over and over, keeping in mind that the chance of them coming clean about all their deep, dark secrets in the first session, or even the first year, are slim to none.

◊◊◊◊◊◊◊◊◊◊◊◊◊◊◊◊◊◊◊◊◊◊◊◊◊◊◊◊◊◊◊◊◊◊◊◊◊

"I was the only female out there in my unit. I had to search the local women since I was the only female. So many of them had bruises and lashes. What was worse is some were even bleeding between their legs. There was genital mutilation; sometimes it was so recent they were still bleeding from it. Not just women, young girls too."

◊◊◊◊◊◊◊◊◊◊◊◊◊◊◊◊◊◊◊◊◊◊◊◊◊◊◊◊◊◊◊◊◊◊◊◊◊

There was a period of time during my college internships when I worked with civilians for about two and a half years.

There's a very big difference between what civilians are willing to voluntarily report about themselves versus what a military member or veteran is willing to report.

I needed the concept of specificity not only to coax out the trauma stories, but also to establish a comfort zone. Specific, blunt questions are more comfortable for veterans than deep sympathy and soft-spokenness. Battle-hardened men and women often do not trust what feels to them like fake sympathy. Concrete questions tend to work better, along with their therapist simply being a human being in the session. Being genuine and real with clients is one of the best ways to work toward earning their trust.

"I estimate about one mortar attack a week on our FOB. I had to ID troops' dead bodies constantly, one to two times a week. On a convoy one time, we also saw a marketplace get blown up. We were ordered not to stop and had to drive by a bunch of dead bodies and people suffering. I wanted to help. One of the hardest parts of it was being called by mourning parents and blamed for the KIAs and deaths by suicide, accusing us (leadership) of killing their children. I stayed quiet and let them blame me. There was nothing I could say that would make it right."

Veterans are also more likely to feel insulted or peeved the moment you give them that look or tone of voice that implies they might be soft, fragile, emotional beings. And you've lost them. But on the opposite end, if you're too professional and sound too "textbooky," once again, you've lost them.

We need not insult someone who has been through military training or war with therapy jargon or asking them how they feel about every little thing. What we need to ask about first are their symptoms, behaviors, and facts about their trauma and how it translates to daily life. Emotions come later, after trust has been built.

Remember, clients do not owe therapists the truth; we must earn that with trust. And, as I've mentioned before, trust takes time.

⊙◇⊙◇⊙◇⊙◇⊙◇⊙◇⊙◇⊙◇⊙◇⊙◇⊙◇⊙◇⊙◇⊙◇⊙◇⊙◇⊙◇⊙◇⊙◇

"I remember it so graphically. Seeing their brains all over the ground and walls. Seeing people I knew but so disfigured, most likely dead on sight. The suicide bomber had killed them instantly. And I couldn't do anything. I couldn't save them. I tried to resuscitate them. I tried so hard to save them but I couldn't do anything. Their faces weren't even there anymore."

⊙◇⊙◇⊙◇⊙◇⊙◇⊙◇⊙◇⊙◇⊙◇⊙◇⊙◇⊙◇⊙◇⊙◇⊙◇⊙◇⊙◇⊙◇⊙◇

As therapists, we must be specific and ask questions directly. If we do not ask specific questions, they may never share their trauma on their own. Trauma has a way of silencing people. And some may feel their trauma is irrelevant to their story, like it is something they have put "behind them" so they can move forward. But it still lurks, sometimes unbeknownst to them. Many of the symptoms and emotions related to trauma can be linked to other diagnoses, making that trauma all the more hidden. These are things like depressed mood, anxiety, anger, a need for control, etc.

While it can be hard to get veterans to seek mental health initially, there are some good perks when it comes to government mental health therapists (DOD and VA). There is no pressure to diagnose quickly in order to bill an insurance company for the mental health session. So Military and veteran mental health professionals who work for the government have the luxury of taking their time and getting the diagnosis right—getting the specifics. But, of course, that remains in conflict with the pressure of the military's mission to provide troops for the front line. Thus, we have one more challenge for military members to overcome as they seek the help they need.

ADJUSTMENT! NOT "READJUSTMENT."

"Silence was crucial to save my fragile mind. And now, my words are meaningless and empty. They aren't really me, just rehearsed. My thoughts were cut off from the world. I didn't know how to speak them. I did what I must to survive. I adapted. But now, I can't go back."

Most people have heard of the term "readjustment." It is used widely in the military world, preached to the majority of active duty members as there is a good chance they will go quickly from one living situation to another, sometimes with little to no warning of the impending change. Readjustment suggests going back—as if someone can return exactly as they were and have things exactly as they used to be. When someone has life-altering experiences such as combat training and war zone experiences, returning to the life they left and the person they used to be isn't possible.

Instead, I talk to clients about the many adjustments they've had in life and how those adjustments have both harmed them and provided them with growth and wisdom. Everyone changes as they go through new experiences. It just so happens that military members go through more drastic life-changing experiences at a more rapid rate than most of their civilian counterparts. If military members and veterans are continuously pressured to "readjust" any time they experience changes in their lives, they are almost guaranteed to become burdened with a sense of shame and failure as the task of readjustment is impossible. No military member or veteran should be put under that type of pressure.

"I had already lost eight people I knew on my last tour. Going back was a death sentence; I was terrified when I got orders to go back. No one even understood that. The majority of my family members and friends spent their days worried about taking my money and trying to get a bunch of things from me, and I was terrified to die."

I like to break the typical life-altering adjustments military members experience into five main phases:

- Phase 1: Civilian world to boot camp
- Phase 2: First duty station
- Phase 3: Deployment (e.g., war zone, expeditionary tour, humanitarian mission)
- Phase 4: Return from the deployment (typically with remaining time on their contract)
- Phase 5: Military to civilian world

When laid out like this, I hope it becomes plain that there is no "readjustment" possible. Someone cannot return to the person they were before Phase 1 ever again. By the time someone gets out of the military, they have most likely gone through four or five major adjustments with minimal time to process the things that happened to them or to process how they feel about the many changes. The military does not give troops time to reflect on their many losses or the identity issues that pop up during these crucial adjustments. With younger troops, sometimes these major adjustments are happening even while their brain is still in development.

Here are a few things to keep in mind regarding the list above:

1. I'm not even including the adjustments and stressors of serving while balancing relationships, marriages, divorces, and kids.
2. Some veterans (especially if they were drafted) never got a Phase 4.

3. Some military members are "lifers," meaning they spend twenty-plus years in the military toward a retirement pension. This typically means multiple duty stations and maybe even multiple deployments (i.e., many more adjustments).

These phases are each challenging in their own way. There is much that can go wrong—or right—in any one of them. But, clinically speaking, we must respect Phase 5 the most (adjustment from a military life to the civilian world). Phase 5 needs a lot of care and attention that we, as a society, are neglecting to give it with veteran suicide typically being higher than any other population throughout the history of the U.S.

There is much for military members to grieve when they get out of the military. From the inside looking out, the military member most likely sees their separation or retirement date as freedom. Most military members have accomplished a great deal in their career and have stepped up to very challenging tasks. Nothing in the civilian world sounds even remotely challenging to them in comparison.

❖❖❖❖❖❖❖❖❖❖❖❖❖❖❖❖❖❖❖❖❖❖❖❖❖❖❖❖❖❖❖❖

"We were there doing cleanup. We were at a dumpsite when over a dozen of the village kids and teens ran up to us and started attacking us. They had knives and bats. Some of them were trying to slice our Achilles tendons. They outnumbered us. We had no choice but to fight them. We took their weapons away as best as we could and we ended up beating them over the heads and slicing at them. Whatever we had to do to survive. I have no doubt we killed some of those kids. My daughter is now their age, and it hurts to imagine it happening to her."

❈❖❖❖❖❖❖❖❖❖❖❖❖❖❖❖❖❖❖❖❖❖❖❖❖❖❖❖❖❖❖❖❖❖❖

So, getting out sometimes hits them fast. Other times it hits them in small, chronic, slow doses. The Phase 5 adjustment is about grieving—grieving the loss of a military identity, loss of a job, loss of a steady paycheck and guaranteed shelter, loss of comradery within a unit, loss of a sense of heightened importance and maybe even adrenaline. The sense of purpose is gone, and everything they were and knew is irrelevant. They must start over, but in an organization that has no familiarity—a world that they do not know how to navigate since they were trained for a military environment.

Military members go from a culture in which everything is planned out, in which their days are structured and they are told exactly what to do and where to be at all times, to a world of absolute freedom. That may sound nice, but it means that no one owes them guidance. People are typically too busy to even see that someone is struggling and in need. The military is a team of people who must be willing to die together; the civilian world is an everyone-for-himself way of life.

Adjusting from military to civilian life is often described as one of the hardest things a veteran has ever done. There are some who have literally re-enlisted because the adjustment was too hard. There are some who stay in as long as they can before voluntarily returning to war zones to feel comfortable again.

Many describe the adjustment as being harder than war. There's no "readjustment" here.

PART II

IDENTITY

THE MISSION CANNOT COME FIRST

*"And what is going to happen when it is all said and done,
everything is gone, and you forgot yourself?"*

I am considered a traitor when I say the mission cannot come
first. "The mission must come first" is all that is preached
when entering any branch of the military. Many ask why the
military doesn't put more focus on the mental well-being of
their troops. To put it simply, an organization that is mission-
oriented cannot also be people-oriented; the two orientations
cannot coincide. Human physical and mental health needs
can—and do—interfere with an ongoing war effort. War is
physically and emotionally taxing, and, inevitably, humans

will suffer attempting to keep up with war efforts whether supporting the war stateside or being in the war itself.

⟡⟡⟡⟡⟡⟡⟡⟡⟡⟡⟡⟡⟡⟡⟡⟡⟡⟡⟡⟡⟡⟡⟡⟡⟡⟡⟡⟡⟡⟡⟡⟡⟡

"There were oil fields as we crossed the border. It was like it was raining acid. A group of men came by and started shooting at us. We were ordered not to shoot back, and this was before we even had Kevlar and helmets issued. We just had to sit there and take it. And that's when I really knew, our own people didn't give a f**k about us."

⟡⟡⟡⟡⟡⟡⟡⟡⟡⟡⟡⟡⟡⟡⟡⟡⟡⟡⟡⟡⟡⟡⟡⟡⟡⟡⟡⟡⟡⟡⟡⟡⟡

My argument against the mission coming first is that, in order to accomplish missions, we need the people. Therefore, people must come first. If your troops are operating at 20 percent due to burnout, you can expect a very poor workday. If, overall, many troops are burnt out, you can expect many to get out of the military after their first enlistment. Then you're left training newbies over and over again, and the ones who did stay in are burnt out from a lack of quality, well-trained coworkers.

A first sergeant once asked my opinion on what I would do if I were in charge of his burnt-out unit while I was briefing him on his platoon's "Unit Needs Assessment" survey. I was taken back. A first sergeant was asking me (an E-4 at the time) for my opinion on the matter?

I told him and the commander that in my mental health career so far, I've noticed just how contagious and toxic poor morale can be. It can turn into a vicious cycle, taking everyone down with it, until you no longer have a functioning unit.

This team needed to make some changes; a burnt-out unit is a risky one.

They ignored my social worker colleague and me, brushing it off as, "Well when I was a young soldier I said the same things they are saying." A couple months later, their entire unit was busted for alcohol consumption while on the job. This was against the rules when overseas in combat, but it's not impossible for them to get their hands on alcohol. Where there's a will, there's a way—and desperation leads to will. I didn't stay long enough to find out what happened to that unit.

0-0-0-0-0-0-0-0-0-0-0-0-0-0-0-0-0-0-0-0-0-0-0-0-0-0-0-0-0

"It's all a blur. I did my job and tried to forget everything else. All I can say is we drove through and disintegrated everyone that was in our path, and buried them under rubble. I saw them in front of us running and alive, and then they were gone. For months and months, hundreds of them."

0-0-0-0-0-0-0-0-0-0-0-0-0-0-0-0-0-0-0-0-0-0-0-0-0-0-0-0-0

I did take some satisfaction in knowing that we were right, but my disappointment in knowing that this pattern is all too common far outweighed the satisfaction. When will leadership acknowledge that they too have a role in the mental well-being of their people? Yes, it is war. Yes, war is hard. But a burnt-out unit is a huge issue, especially in a war.

Too many clients have described themselves as disposable, pawns on a chessboard, used and abused, etc. Many have reported that the sacrifices they made were not worth what they earned from their military service.

The "mission comes first" mentality says that numbers mean everything, and the moment someone can no longer be a number for them in war, they are no longer wanted or useful. They are tossed aside like yesterday's garbage. When a military member is profiled and considered "non-deployable" due to injury or mental illness, there is often little incentive for commanders to want to retain them.

⊙◇⊙◇⊙◇⊙◇⊙◇⊙◇⊙◇⊙◇⊙◇⊙◇⊙◇⊙◇⊙◇⊙◇⊙◇⊙◇⊙◇◇⊙

"I was being medevaced lying right under another injured guy. I felt a lot of drips on my leg and soon realized he was bleeding all over me. I go to check on him and see he's bleeding to death. I start to fix his tourniquet and before I know it I'm being pulled off and denied to help a fellow soldier. I insisted and fought and fought until they injected me to put me to sleep."

⊙◇⊙◇⊙◇⊙◇⊙◇⊙◇⊙◇⊙◇⊙◇⊙◇⊙◇⊙◇⊙◇⊙◇⊙◇⊙◇⊙◇◇⊙

During deployment, I came across a soldier who had lost his infant child while he was away. Naturally, he and his wife were both devastated, and he was permitted grievance. They sent him home for a short period of time to attend the funeral… and then sent him right back to war. My social work colleague wrote a letter to command explaining why this soldier was not in the right mental state to continue a combat deployment, and, thankfully, they listened and sent him back home. But the fact that that letter even had to be written in the first place is a huge problem. The focus on the mission coming first above all else is toxic to the mental well-being of troops.

I said it when I was serving, and I say it post-service too: If the military wants high-functioning soldiers who never need breaks and can always work hard with no periods of exhaustion, they should have hired robots instead. This isn't to say that all military units are toxic or that the military purposely damages their employees, but the theme of emotional damage that the military does contribute to needs to be highlighted and explored in order to do better for our traumatized service members and veterans.

SUPERHUMAN

"I climbed a thousand mountains, and then that hill stopped me in my tracks."

A military member is held to extremely high expectations, and they are bound by contract to live up to those expectations. Some of those expectations are the same as those all working class adults must hold to: waking up, going to work, being on time, being accountable, and listening to your boss.

But on top of the usual expectations, military members will most likely have mandatory physical training (PT) three to five times per week either before or after work, so just tack that onto the typical duty day. In addition, their annual performance reports aren't just about their work performance.

Often, they include a review of how someone is volunteering or doing things for their own self-improvement beyond their military job.

Volunteering and/or going to school become common standard expectations, but this also depends on the branch and unit of the service member. A civilian employer is typically only concerned with how someone is doing their job, nothing more. Just do your job and you may have whatever life you want to have outside of work. A military supervisor, however, would likely expect you to do your job to the best of your ability every day, do PT three to five times per week, have an amazing PT test score, volunteer, be enrolled in college part-time, and make appearances at what the military has coined "mandatory fun time."

"I did not want to go into the gunner's turret in the Humvee that day. My friend offered to do it for me. I was in the Humvee behind him on the convoy. An IED blew up the bridge right above their Humvee in front of us. I saw my buddy in the turret get decapitated from the car that fell off the bridge. He took my place and then he died because of it."

There is no overtime pay, and there are no real limits on how many hours command can make their troops work. There are supposed limits, but who's counting? And who's regulating these? And if these rules are broken, who dares blow the whistle? An active duty military member cannot sue the

DOD, regardless of the emotional or physical damage they are subjected to. Some clients have reported shifts so long they used meth or popped pills just to stay awake. Some have reported near-death experiences falling asleep behind the wheel from being so tired.

The military puts young, inexperienced troops through many hardships and many adjustments and stressors, and the organization is unforgiving of mistakes. As difficult as this lifestyle may sound, human beings do adapt and "overcome." Well, most do. The ones who do not adapt get weeded out quickly. Some get removed even as early as boot camp. After some time for adaptation, the superhuman troop starts to believe this lifestyle is normal. They start to believe that anyone who could not adapt, like they could, is weak and whiny. Those who can't adapt don't belong in "their military" if they can't hack it.

<hr>

"We were on a patrol with their country's national army. All of a sudden some enemy combatants popped out to attack us. As soon as they did, the allies turned out to also be the enemy. They turned on us and shot at us too. There were also mortars going off from a distance. Complete ambush. We fought back and ended up killing them all, but three of my friends in my unit were killed. After the attack was done, we had to carry their bodies back down the mountain with us."

<hr>

What military members are expected to endure is not the norm—and it is not healthy. But, for many, it is worth it for the many benefits they earn with at least thirty-six months of honorable active duty service: 'free' college (GI Bill), monthly allowance while in school, a VA home loan (sometimes zero down), free medical and dental for them and their family while serving.

But, eventually, given enough time, traumas, burnout, and aging, every human finds their limitations, because it's a pace that cannot go on forever. And what happens then? Will the veteran accept those limitations? Will they grieve their losses? Will they create new, reasonable goals that are within the scope of what they can do now? Or will they keep trying to be superhuman with a very human mind and body? There's a chance they hurt and yearn for the person they were—and feel shame about who they've become.

However, slowing down is necessary. We are regular humans, after all. But because of the high work pace military members are subjected to, high expectations of themselves follow. Does those expectations stop after the military service ends? The need to keep busy, the need to continue missions and carry on with purpose and a sense of urgency? Although the body might be ready to slow down and take a load off, the mind may still feel the urge to stay in military mode at a military pace. This can be overwhelming, and it rarely translates to the civilian world. Sometimes veterans may be taken advantage of in work settings because of their fast pace and willingness to continue being job-oriented.

"I told them to dig trenches to hide/sleep in. I was the only one that night that wanted to do it for myself. We went to sleep, fell under attack, and I was the only one in my platoon that survived that day."

In other cases, veterans may be convinced to slow down with proper guidance. My first internship supervisor post-military service threw me off. She often encouraged me to take breaks. She took pity on me. "Oh my goodness, Elisa, you are so busy. You're in college and interning and you still go to the gym and you do your weekends with the military! (During college, I transferred from active duty to Air Force reserves). Are you okay? Do you need a break?" She said this to me every week, and I often just gave her strange looks as I responded that I was fine.

I could not understand where the pity was coming from. Since when did a supervisor care about my personal needs? It was both odd and comforting not to be held to high expectations anymore. I've had multiple civilian supervisors since this incident, and they have all told me the same thing: "Slow down, you might burn out." That was the common theme of the conversations. I had roughly five supervisors during my six-year active duty Air Force enlistment. None of the military supervisors gave me that feedback. I was a slow learner and was very much punished for it. When I eventually transformed into a superhuman, I was often pressured to keep the pace up.

Superhuman is not an official term, but when I choose to use it when speaking with veteran clients, many have identified with the term. They were once highly efficient and functional human beings, and they are now in the civilian world doing a job and/or going to school, many with the sense that what they are doing and working toward is not as important as their mission in the military. Just as difficult as building a high work ethic is undoing this habit and developing the skills to recognize when and if we need to slow down. There are no more superhuman expectations and demands after military service, and that is okay.

BEING "RESILIENT"

"I am fighting, every day, just to get myself back. Not even to succeed or thrive, just to live. We are strongest when we seem weak. People will see "helpless." What they won't see is the millions of battles you are fighting within yourself, just to be okay."

Resiliency is not what people think it is. I've heard the comment many times that "some people are just more resilient than others."

Okay, that tells me nothing.

The military gives presentations on resiliency that also told me nothing. "Be resilient. Overcome things. Be strong! Get through it!" Where's the actual advice on how to overcome?

And what about how to overcome not in the best of times, but in the worst of times?

They call resiliency "the ability to bounce back" after an adverse situation. But who can give us answers on how to bounce back after seeing people get blown up? After being sexually assaulted? After going to war and coming back home and reintegrating with minimal time off. Or even going from a traumatic childhood straight into the demanding organization that is the military? When there's an endless series of adverse situations, partnered with a lack of support and a stigma against getting help, how do we keep it together? Are we as okay as we seem? Or are we pretending and playing the game to look strong?

"I did whatever I could do to help them. The medics told me to move the f**k aside and stay out of their way. So I just did what I could do. I picked up organs off of the floor, mopped up blood. I carried litters and watched as bodies fell apart. I saw someone that I had just met a week ago, half of his face was blown off."

True resiliency stems from a strong support system, especially in childhood. As adverse situations come, kids and young adults with strong support systems have the ability to bounce back because they have actual options, places to recover, get help, or take breaks. But for those with no help or abusive households, every adverse situation makes them more weathered down, with nothing and no one to keep them afloat.

Eventually, the chronic lack of a support system and love teaches a young person that recovery isn't an option. The world is hard, and trying will only tire them out. They're in a hole, they will stay there as they always have, and they simply do not have the luxury of help. They suffer alone. It's not laziness; it's hopelessness. It's not an inherent weakness; it's chronic pain and suffering.

In addition, PTSD of any kind can break down a person who maybe originally had a healthy amount of resiliency. To put it simply, someone who has suffered from childhood trauma before the military, sexual trauma, or combat trauma in the military will appear "less resilient" than their non-traumatized counterparts. The non-traumatized often appear to be the more functional and less dramatic people, the ones who can keep their s**t together. PTSD often makes for the behavior and appearance of an "unstable" person who cannot handle day-to-day duty. Leadership often believes they are malingerers. Others shame them, and the sufferer will believe their lies. Those who are suffering become outcasts for their perceived lack of resiliency and are sometimes even bullied.

There is so much in life that is about the luck of the draw, but we don't typically see it that way. Having good parents, having a safe and fun military career, not getting assaulted or exposed to trauma…that's all privilege.

The opportunity to build healthy resiliency and have a lot of support is a privilege.

Then, of course, there are people who went through the worst of traumas and still remain standing, and those individuals might despise anyone who appears to have had it easier than them. They say things like, "I went through a miserable life and I'm not whining." The problem is, they're most likely not okay either, but their defenses are high, and the mind plays tricks to convince people they are fine. But family and friends will see the buildup of symptoms continue.

◇◇◇◇◇◇◇◇◇◇◇◇◇◇◇◇◇◇◇◇◇◇◇◇◇◇◇◇◇◇◇◇◇◇

"I remember the only way out of a hot zone was to drive over dozens of dead bodies that were surrounding us. We drove as fast as we could and saw all the limbs and heads flying upward as we made our way out of danger."

◇◇◇◇◇◇◇◇◇◇◇◇◇◇◇◇◇◇◇◇◇◇◇◇◇◇◇◇◇◇◇◇◇◇

Most people have heard of the nature versus nurture debate. Well, resiliency has a lot to do with nurture—the environment, including people. How well are we treated in a world that's often so unpredictable? How can we compare levels of resiliency? Is it that one person is stronger than another? Or maybe one person has had an easier life than another? Or maybe one person has more help and support than another? I personally do not think it's fair to describe people as "non-resilient," because there is no true template for resiliency. There are only people, typically wanting life and trying their best, faced with inevitable hardships, using whatever they have mentally and physically to roll with the punches.

If support is what the non-resilient are deprived of, usually it's support and healing they need in order to start gaining a healthy level of resilience. This is often where therapists come in. By the time clients get to me, not only are they weathered down and suffering from multiple symptoms, but their self-esteem is also shot. They feel like they are wrong to even need to seek help in the first place. They feel ashamed that they couldn't keep it together like their "healthier" coworkers and peers.

"I had to play god. They had me come into the intelligence unit anytime they needed me to call the shots and to justify the killing for the drone pilots. They had to make sure it didn't violate the rules of engagement. I had to make that call; it was on me. And sometimes they didn't care what I said at all; it was just checking a box."

When I reflect with my clients on all of the ways in which they were disadvantaged, it starts to open their eyes. A big weight is lifted, and they are relieved. It's important for people to know and understand what they are actually responsible for, what to hold themselves accountable for, and what is truly not their fault. The "non-resilient" ones are the ones who grew up deprived of nurturing and resources. PTSD can also erode someone's ability to bounce back, as the symptoms are often far too extreme for the defenses someone initially entered the military with. Sufferers of mental illness need something stronger than your average "resiliency skills," and that does not mean that they lack strength altogether.

CULTURE SHOCK

"When we focus so hard on an individual's behavior, we forget to evaluate what's causing it. We would rather judge the behavior than figure out the complex emotional pain behind it, and when that is done, change is impossible."

People always ask how hard it can possibly be to transition from military life to civilian life. I believe in order to grasp the answer, one must first know a little bit about military culture. And those mandated equal opportunity briefings in the civilian workforce should include military culture in order to help make a more cohesive workplace when civilians and veterans are forced to work together in a shared space.

I explain to many veteran clients what it means to "militarize" their external environment post-service. Often they do this subconsciously with the goal of establishing a comfort zone and having a livelihood that feels familiar and encourages the habits picked up during their service. Veterans can militarize their jobs, their classroom experience, or even their household. Sometimes the military may remain the root of their identity altogether.

So, how does a veteran militarize a civilian workspace? Some habits may include micromanaging and believing they must complete "the mission" at all costs, even if the job is something simple and does not have the consequence of death if it's not done right away. They often see anyone who is not up to the task at hand (their civilian counterparts) as lazy and incompetent. Before you know it, veterans have insulted their coworkers, who have insulted them back, and the work environment may or may not become hostile depending on how badly someone is triggered.

Obviously, it does not always get this dramatic. Sometimes veterans have a hard time communicating the smaller things that are difficult and why to civilian employers. For example, I eventually had to admit to one of my civilian social work supervisors, "I do not know how to not take orders." His flexibility and leniency with how I worked and when I showed up was extremely confusing and hard for me to wrap my head around.

⬦⬦⬦⬦⬦⬦⬦⬦⬦⬦⬦⬦⬦⬦⬦⬦⬦⬦⬦⬦⬦⬦⬦⬦⬦⬦⬦⬦⬦⬦⬦⬦

"All I wanted to do through that deployment was run away, every second of every day. People are shooting at us constantly, losing my friends constantly everywhere I looked, left and right. Seeing how they die, not knowing if I was going to be next. Everything in me mentally and physically told me to run from this. But there is nowhere to run to. We were literally surrounded by death."

When evaluating how both cultures operate, it's important to be fair and neutral. I explain to veterans the things civilians do better, because what seems like "lazy" to a veteran may actually be viewed as a steady pace. A civilian leaving right at 5:00 pm isn't lazy; rather, they are placing priority on their own self-care. Civilians are not on duty 24/7—and neither are veterans once they return to the civilian world. I encourage them to leave at 5:00 pm if they only get paid until 5:00 pm. If everyone else takes breaks, they should take breaks too. And try not to fight it. There were most likely many times while in the military they would have killed for a break.

As for college, veterans might militarize the classroom by sitting in an area where they have a view of the exits and others around them, so they can scan for danger. They may want to be close to the exit for a quick getaway if they are triggered. Veterans may have a hard time if a teacher gives too much creative freedom as they are used to being given exact orders (instructions) for their next mission (college assignments).

And militarizing a household might look something like this: Kids have very strict rules and expectations. Kids may not be allowed to make many mistakes, as the world is very dangerous; therefore, they cannot afford to make mistakes.

Sometimes the spouse and kids are seen as incompetent in the eyes of a veteran because they are sheltered and living in a bubble. They do not seem to understand the true dangers of the world. The reality is that other members of the household most likely were not in a war zone, so it makes sense that they are not as vigilant.

◇◇◇◇◇◇◇◇◇◇◇◇◇◇◇◇◇◇◇◇◇◇◇◇◇◇◇◇◇◇◇◇

"I was on a carrier ship. Seeing people getting their limbs torn off or crushed whenever an accident happened. A guy's foot was run over by one of the jets that had just landed. A piece of equipment had snapped and chopped off another guy's hand. We worked insanely long shifts, sometimes days at a time. I had designated areas where I went just to hide from everything. The military turned me into a drug addict."

◇◇◇◇◇◇◇◇◇◇◇◇◇◇◇◇◇◇◇◇◇◇◇◇◇◇◇◇◇◇◇◇

Naturally, the civilian family usually fights against the instincts of the veteran. If you have not gone to a war zone, your sense of safety will be very different than someone's who has. No one is wrong here. Both parties may need more compassion and empathy as they learn about each other's wants and needs or as the family dynamics change post-war and post-service.

I've had many veterans tell me about their family members using the classic line: "You aren't in the military anymore!" I'm never surprised to hear that one. But whether someone is still serving or not, those experiences have shaped and changed their entire worldview. There is no going back to who they were.

All in all, this disconnect can be very painful when a veteran gets out of the military. They are typically around people they have known their entire life, but it's as if they are now strangers. The military culture changes every individual who serves, and that culture trickles down into their families, workspaces, spiritual lives, and social dynamics. It truly is a culture shock, and feeling alienated often follows.

ALIENATION

"I need to understand this void and why absolutely nothing and no one can fill it."

To paint the picture right, imagine plucking a random person from the civilian world and placing them in a military unit. To give it even more of a twist, imagine this civilian did not endure boot camp training or even tech school. They are just thrown right into a duty station and expected to get to work. They must learn dress and appearance regulations on their own, chain of command, and who to salute or not to salute outside. They have to adapt to the workplace environment, no matter how tedious and crude it may seem.

On top of this, the civilian will have to learn to work overtime for no extra pay, and they often have their weekends taken away from them at a moment's notice. They have to adapt to the idea of being forced to live wherever the government decides to place them, no ifs, ands, or buts. If they complain, they will be laughed at, ridiculed, and invalidated. They will be accused of being entitled and clueless.

We wouldn't do that to a civilian; it wouldn't be right. However, this scenario is very much like what a veteran experiences when they get out of the military. They are alien to the civilian world. In the scenario we just imagined, the civilian would be alien to the military world. Is it possible for that civilian to adapt? Maybe. But is it easy? Absolutely not.

In the last chapter, there were examples of how the cultures of the military and civilian worlds differ and clash. This chapter focuses on the loneliness those differences can cause. Our veterans are typically alienated in the civilian world, and it seems they always have been. There's a specific field in anthropology called ethnography in which an anthropologist lives and immerses themself into a completely different culture than the one they grew up in, and they document their entire experience. It's a very fascinating career path and, I'll admit, I was almost tempted to switch majors because of it.

❀❀❀❀❀❀❀❀❀❀❀❀❀❀❀❀❀❀❀❀❀❀❀❀❀❀❀❀❀❀❀

"I lost my glasses, so they sent me off for a few days to make sure I got new ones. When I flew back to where my unit was, from the sky I saw my entire platoon laying in body bags. They all got killed while I was away getting my new glasses."

❁❁❁❁❁❁❁❁❁❁❁❁❁❁❁❁❁❁❁❁❁❁❁❁❁❁❁❁❁❁❁❁❁❁❁

The more I work with veterans and reflect on my own experiences in the military and civilian worlds, the more I realize that military members essentially do what ethnographers do when they transition to the civilian sector, but with the addition of the shock factor. How could I possibly be more shocked and out of place moving to NYC than I felt in Afghanistan? NYC is in my country, the country I have lived in my entire life. Yet, something was different.

What's different isn't the civilian world; it's us as former members of the military. We become different due to the military lifestyle. The dynamics of alienation are very complex and intricate, but they all matter. Every veteran client I have worked with has expressed this feeling of alienation. Every day they serve takes them further and further from the people and the society they once knew. By the time they get out of the military, they are a stranger to everyone, and everyone is a stranger to them. The old pleasantries they used to enjoy no longer cut it. People do not feel relatable anymore. And that lost human connection is not only unpleasant, but extremely harmful since it is crucial for social and emotional health to have human connections. No longer a member of the military, but also not really a "normal" civilian, trying to find a place as a veteran.

Many bring up the military's transition assistance program, which is often described by veterans as a "joke" and not very helpful. My personal transition assistance before I separated from the military consisted of creating my new budget for my move to NYC, as well as a resume for the civilian sector. My resume was approved, although it was two and a half pages and in military bullet point format. And my budget was completely inaccurate since I had no clue how expensive NYC really was.

Needless to say, I was unprepared, shocked, and felt like a fool. My post-service year of complaining on social media or confiding to civilian friends was often greeted with cynicism topped with a significant lack of empathy. I suppose because things like budgeting and creating a resume were easy and commonsensical in their world, they couldn't understand why I was having a hard time and complaining on top of it. I was as alienated as most veterans.

٥٥٥

"The plane crashed. I'm not even sure why. But my section was tasked to go on a search and recovery mission. Everyone was dead. I spent that day picking up burnt bodies, seeing detached body parts all over."

٥٥٥

So, how do we move past the alienation? Or rather, how do we adjust with minimal pain and loneliness? Patience is the biggest virtue, and shame the biggest enemy. We all learned how to be military members with time and training. It is a difficult task to learn how to be a civilian. And, like the constant trial and errors throughout military enlistment, it will take a lot of time. Do not expect otherwise.

I often joke that if we had a civilian boot camp to prep military members for getting out of the service, it would look something like this:

- Do not be early! It wastes self-care time.
- Don't expect orders; take orders or give orders. You have freedom of will, as does everyone else.
- Deeply explore and research your healthcare options, make your own appointments, and go!
- Communication involves both listening and speaking. You can speak now; you have a voice.
- Express emotions. They are healthy and no longer forbidden.
- Veteran is one of your identities, but it is not the only one. Refrain from pulling rank.
- Remember that your civilian counterparts were not trained to be war machines. Have patience with them and model them when it comes to work pace and self-care.
- You can do what you want and go where you want; you do not need special permission.
- No one is responsible for you and making sure you have your s**t together. It's all on you now, and most people do not have the time or desire to care.

We have every right to embrace our veteran identities, but also remember that getting out means adapting to a different world. The more we fight that adaptation, the more we appear alien to our new civilian world.

WAR ZONE ADAPTATION

"Being forced, controlled, and coerced is a lifestyle that humans are very much capable of adapting to. They can sustain life in chaos and, upon absence of it, find themselves lost."

War zone adaptation and war zone traumas are unique in their own right, and I want to give due diligence to this topic.

First of all, many things can cause PTSD. Most people understand that you do not need to go to war to develop PTSD, and you also might get through a war zone experience without developing PTSD.

But I do want to cover the uniqueness of PTSD when it does stem from a war zone environment and combat exposure. In the "normal" world, a trauma might be a terrible car accident, losing a loved one suddenly, an assault, a serious medical condition and hospitalization, etc. After a trauma happens in the "normal" world, someone is granted some time off if they have gone through something horrific. They might get some bereavement days, or use sick leave. There is often a support system of people who help them get through an awful period of time. There is some type of empathy or sympathy. Self-care is stressed.

War traumas, on the other hand, often come in the most raw and true forms of life-or-death situations—in the middle of firefights, being bombed, seeing another member of the team get killed right in front of you. As terrifying as it is, war is happening. And war must go on. It's either war goes on, or you might die next. There are no days off, no bereavement time. In fact, the trauma can happen right at the beginning or in the middle of a deployment, with any return home far from sight.

⬦⬦⬦⬦⬦⬦⬦⬦⬦⬦⬦⬦⬦⬦⬦⬦⬦⬦⬦⬦⬦⬦⬦⬦⬦⬦⬦⬦⬦⬦⬦⬦

"We used to get drop offs at our FOB every so often. Locals that helped us, that the terrorists would pick up and make an example of. They would drop them off right out front by the tower guards at our base with their tongues and ears stapled to their faces."

⬦⬦⬦⬦⬦⬦⬦⬦⬦⬦⬦⬦⬦⬦⬦⬦⬦⬦⬦⬦⬦⬦⬦⬦⬦⬦⬦⬦⬦⬦⬦⬦

How does someone go on? How do they keep fighting after being severely traumatized?

The most common defense mechanisms include psychological numbing, minimizing or normalizing the situation, suppressing their emotions at all costs, and trying to dissociate from their reality. Many describe going into a muscle memory mode during war moments that are highly adrenalized in order to complete whatever tasks are right in front of them.

In the short run, the military member is doing what is best in the midst of a combat trauma so that they may stay alive. But in the long run, without breaks or opportunities to grieve and process, their PTSD symptoms become more severe and chronic until they are out of service and actually afforded the opportunity and time to heal (which, as I've addressed elsewhere in this book, is a big if).

This is why military members and veterans are more likely to experience what professionals call "PTSD with delayed onset." As long as they remain in defense mode with a ton of work that still needs to be done, they aren't truly processing anything. They are still reacting in a state of hypervigilance, which will continue to protect them in a combat zone. There are even some who voluntarily return to war so that their symptoms may feel normal again, as I mentioned in another chapter. When the mind and body are adapted to a war zone, being in war starts to feel like the norm. Meanwhile, being back home post-war might feel discomforting.

⬦⬦⬦⬦⬦⬦⬦⬦⬦⬦⬦⬦⬦⬦⬦⬦⬦⬦⬦⬦⬦⬦⬦⬦⬦⬦⬦⬦⬦⬦⬦⬦⬦⬦⬦

"I remember us standing around in one of the local villages watching a public beheading. This man had molested one of the girls supposedly. They beheaded him with a machete. I'll never forget the sound of the thud when the head hits the ground, or the fluttering of his eyes."

⬦⬦⬦⬦⬦⬦⬦⬦⬦⬦⬦⬦⬦⬦⬦⬦⬦⬦⬦⬦⬦⬦⬦⬦⬦⬦⬦⬦⬦⬦⬦⬦⬦⬦⬦

To be mentally and physiologically adapted to a war zone while living in the civilian world is one of the most confusing and hindering feelings. There isn't an off switch. It takes a lot of time to adapt to war, and it can take a lifetime to adapt to being home. Despite home being safer for the most part, there are triggers everywhere.

Something as simple as seeing, hearing, feeling, or smelling something remotely similar to the war zone can return veterans to fight-or-flight mode. Memory is powerful, and our senses are meant to tell the memory and body, "Hey! You might be in danger again. This feels familiar!" Because of the PTSD symptoms, daily life can turn into work, preventing veterans from actual enjoyment and being present in the moment. Simple things like hobbies or errands start to feel like walking into a battlefield all over again. It takes a lot of effort to self-soothe after the body and mind are triggered. Some people report dealing with hours or days of anxiety and depression after trauma triggers, which is very hindering for anyone's daily lifestyle. But the majority of traumatized veterans would never dare admit to these types of daily obstacles.

There is no invention that allows us to go into the brain, erase trauma memories, and leave everything else—all the good memories—still intact. Many describe their PTSD never feeling "cured." Rather, with enough therapy, healthy coping mechanisms, and sometimes medication, they learn to manage their triggers and symptoms better. As I've said before, everyone who can should get treatment. I tell all of my war veteran clients, "You are not crazy, and you are not wrong. You were traumatized."

⊕·◈·◎

"We responded to so many injured and wounded. One time it was an entire bus of civilians that got blown up by a large VBIED. By the time I arrived to the scene, it was the mother with her legs blown off and her baby already dead. The father was crying as he looked at them."

⊕·◈·◎

There are a significant number of veterans who have been to war and are still in disbelief when they get a PTSD diagnosis. Many still believe receiving that diagnosis means they are weak. However, those who suffer from war zone traumas and have lived to tell the stories are some of the strongest and bravest people I have ever known or worked with as they work their way through being adapted for a war zone.

STOLEN POWER

"I was silenced, my thoughts condemned, my feelings ignored. My happiness was deemed irrelevant, and therefore my rage and pain suppressed. There is a reason I cannot trust again."

Would you believe that one of your best buddies and most incredible coworkers is a rapist? Actually think about that. Pick one of your favorites coworkers in the world and imagine being told that they were accused of rape. Who would you believe? Could it be true? Most likely you would look at the stranger who accused this friend with skepticism. It just couldn't be true. They would never...right?

If you supervised this coworker who's currently being accused, along with this new troop who's accusing him, who are you siding with? Do you let the investigation run its course and choose to believe whatever the decision is? What if you had the opportunity to stop the investigation and save your friend, because this troop who accused them seems sketchy and they throw themself at everyone anyways? This new troop is also always late and has a poor work ethic, which makes them seem untrustworthy.

After someone is assaulted, there is a big chance they will go to their frontline supervisor first in order to report it. This is where things can get messy, especially if the perpetrator is in the same unit. A unit is supposed to get the sexual assault response coordinator (SARC) involved. And, in a perfect world, there would be a non-biased investigation. The troop can go straight to the SARC in secret, but, most likely, the supervisor will still find out, as they will need to know why that troop is missing duty. Accountability is shoved down the throats of military members. Supervisors have a right to know where troops are at all times. As the popular expression goes: "We are on duty 24/7."

⬦⬦⬦⬦⬦⬦⬦⬦⬦⬦⬦⬦⬦⬦⬦⬦⬦⬦⬦⬦⬦⬦⬦⬦⬦⬦⬦⬦⬦⬦⬦⬦⬦

"I was riding in the back of the convoy. We had only been there a month. And then, as we were riding, we started to come near a couple of the local women. Then the men beside me took out their grenade launcher. I saw them shoot and kill the women with it. Then they turned to me and said,

'If you say anything we will shoot you motherf**er. Do you understand?' I still carry guilt for not saying anything."

❂◦❂

For the longest time, the issue in the military has been that so many of these investigations are internal. It ends up being a matter of who is the commander's or supervisor's favorite. There also may be few to no witnesses and then it also turns into a matter of "he said, she said." Or "he said, he said, she said, she said." Everyone has bias—the coworkers, the supervisors, the first sergeants, the commanders, the potential witnesses. They are all military members, and there's a higher likelihood that they know both the accused and the accuser. It's a small base, and a small military.

Many will not report sexual harassment or sexual assault in the military because they're already aware of this bias and the stigma. There have also been many who have reported their assault, only to witness a toxic unit sweep it under the rug to protect the accused. Many troops get to the investigation process only to be accused of being a liar. Some may win their case, but they will most likely suffer from PTSD for the rest of their lives, which is not really a win.

The symptoms of PTSD will manifest and create someone who is angry, who cannot trust another soul, and who hates the DOD if they did nothing to help post-assault. Or, even worse, the DOD may have traumatized them further post-assault.

Another thing to consider is the reaction assault survivors often get. Combat trauma solicits empathy and is associated with heroics. The people in a troop's unit are supposed to be trustworthy and have their back, but sexual trauma is met with skepticism and shame. "Well did you give them any reason to think they had a chance with you?" "Were you in a safe area?" "You should have had a battle buddy with you. Those are the rules! Why were you alone?" "You were alone with that person at their place so…what did you expect?"

◇◦◇

"I got raped twice in the military, both by higher ranking male coworkers. I reported both incidents to higher-ups. The first time they said it didn't even happen. The second time they blamed me and kept insisting it was my fault. I was young and didn't even know my options back then. And back in those days there wasn't a sexual assault response person to go to."

◇◦◇

These are the things someone who has not been assaulted says to validate that they are safe. It's their security blanket. Assault won't happen to them because they don't put themselves in dangerous situations where they could get assaulted. Right? Wrong. Every person in the world has been in multiple scenarios where they could have been assaulted.

If someone has ever gotten a ride home from a friend while intoxicated, they could have gotten assaulted. If someone set their drink down at a house party, no matter the size or who's there, they could have gotten assaulted. If someone goes grocery shopping a little late and the parking lot is pretty empty, they could have gotten assaulted. If you are a living and breathing person at this very second, you could get assaulted.

The only difference between someone who has been assaulted and someone who hasn't is luck. Those who haven't been assaulted are lucky to have had trustworthy friends their entire lives. They are lucky not to have met paths with a stranger looking for their next victim at a convenient place and time.

◊-◊

"They hated me for being a woman, that's the only guess I can make. They hazed me nonstop, made me roll in mud, called me s**t bag, and constantly screamed at me. Some of them made sexual advances at me on the regular. They knew where I stayed too. One of them came to my room, one of the few that pretended to be my friend. He started to make advances and slipped his hands under my shorts. I hesitated and froze, but he still kept going. I stayed quiet and convinced myself..."If I do not fight it, than it isn't assault." Afterwards, he spread rumors that we had 'consensual sex.' It was humiliating."

◊-◊

Both men and women in the military are getting assaulted, and the numbers are roughly the same for both genders. There are more men than women in the military, so women are still proportionately at higher risk. The chances of a troop reporting the assault, it being taken seriously, and the outcome working in the victim's favor are very low. There is a rising trend of victims being wrongfully diagnosed by military mental health clinics (sometimes because they didn't report the assault) and pushed out of the military due to "adjustment disorders" or "personality disorders." Again, sexual trauma makes for a troop who appears to out of line. They are seen as having anger or attitude problems because of their many PTSD triggers post-assault that they are often not getting help for.

There has been a history and trend of sexual assault victims being pushed out too soon with little to no benefits. There are some who weather the storm and stay in the military to discharge honorably, but the symptoms of PTSD continue getting worse. Their mental and physical health deteriorates rapidly. Military sexual trauma (MST) is now getting the recognition it deserves, and services have expanded accordingly. Still, a lot of work and education must take place to start returning military members' stolen power.

"ISMS"

"We are not only manipulated into believing right from wrong, but also how we should feel in any given situation. How we should look, how we should treat others, and what or who should be valued. When I make a choice, I don't even know if it's my own anymore."

I tell many clients and friends that beneath every uniform, beneath every job title, beneath every rank and status, there lies a human being. And human beings are fallible. They will never be perfect, and some will say and do messed-up things. Some have biases and ill intentions. Some use their power to violate and coerce.

There is every "ism" in the military that there is in the civilian world. The uniform does not make us above or immune to this fact. Military members have, in both the past and present, committed and experienced acts of racism, sexism, classism, homophobia, etc.

I have heard so many firsthand accounts, both in sessions with clients and in stories from close friends from the military about the presence of these "isms." Sometimes they come from a state of ignorance; others stem from real hate.

The military brings people together from all over the place. Then it merges and lumps those random people together in work units. The military doesn't care if you haven't worked with or met people of color before. They expect troops to get used to it. They do not care if you're sexist. They expect troops to learn to work with women in uniform. They also don't think about how potentially hazardous the merge can be for a marginalized person. They put rules in place to prevent discrimination, such as the equal opportunity office and zero tolerance policies for these "isms." But the real issue is that if someone is the target of discrimination, and these policies fall through or get ignored, the person who is targeted is truly stuck. They are under contract. Who knows when or if they will be able to relocate to another duty station?

◊◊

"Every day they harassed me. They told me they had condoms with my name on it. Touched me inappropriately. They threatened to assault me on the regular. I finally felt like I had to give in and give my supervisor what he wanted. It was either they take it from me, or I pretend it was my idea. Then maybe it won't feel like assault…"

⬦⬦⬦⬦⬦⬦⬦⬦⬦⬦⬦⬦⬦⬦⬦⬦⬦⬦⬦⬦⬦⬦⬦⬦⬦⬦⬦⬦⬦⬦⬦⬦⬦⬦⬦⬦

Change is slow, and just because laws and policies change doesn't mean that people change. The changes don't mean people's mindsets and biases have changed. Law is only paper. I've had the privilege of working with veterans who served during the Korean War, Vietnam, and Desert Storm. As units began to desegregate troops and ordered military members to treat people of color and women equally, the clash was brutal on many minority and female service members. I have heard of so many instances of micro-aggressions, pure aggressive acts, and hatred toward anyone who was 'different'. To this day, discrimination still exists in some units, but is it now very well-hidden. Being a target of discrimination in a work unit is very traumatic. Going to work every day with a bunch of people who hate you and threaten you is very traumatic.

⬦⬦⬦⬦⬦⬦⬦⬦⬦⬦⬦⬦⬦⬦⬦⬦⬦⬦⬦⬦⬦⬦⬦⬦⬦⬦⬦⬦⬦⬦⬦⬦⬦⬦⬦⬦

"My initial "hale & farewell" to the unit involved them (white military members) putting a noose around my neck. There were bystanders that did nothing for me, they just watched. Later, when I confronted people about the noose hanging up on a wall during an awards ceremony, they refused to take it down and described it as "tradition". Being the only black military member in my shop, I experienced many microaggressions. I had to repeatedly tell an NCO to stop calling me "boy". Punishments for black military members throughout the squadron were often more severe than our white counterparts. When I was pushing myself to cross train and doing PT with my ruck sack on, some white men that were driving by in their pickup truck pointed a loaded pistol at me as they drove by. This was the norm for my entire six-year career, stationed at a racist base in a racist town.

❉❉❉❉❉❉❉❉❉❉❉❉❉❉❉❉❉❉❉❉❉❉❉❉❉❉❉❉❉❉❉❉❉

Fast-forward to my generation of service in 2010 when "don't ask, don't tell" was repealed and gay service members were finally allowed to openly serve without fear of getting kicked out or harassed. I enlisted in 2008, so I was two years into my career at this point, a low-ranking airman who kept my mouth shut and tried to stay below the radar. We had already been ordered not to discuss politics or get in debates while at work and in uniform. Yet, my opinionated coworkers couldn't help themselves. I had a section chief going on and on about how service members being openly gay was awful for the military work environment. He talked about how it's "not in the Bible," so gay is wrong. He was frustrated that I was not equally outraged, but, in fact, happy for gay service members.

Another male coworker complained about how it would make boot camp weird, as if there weren't already gay people in boot camp. There were roughly four or five lesbians in my boot camp flight, and none of them touched me inappropriately. (Yes, gay people understand consent too.)

In the past couple of years, the transgender debate has also been in full force. It's the new hot topic. The most common argument I hear is that the military shouldn't have to pay for sex change surgeries. (So, I guess we're assuming all transgender people want surgeries.)

It hit me that these things must have been similar to what was being said when women were finally approved to enlist. I can just imagine the talk and questions: "What about when they get pregnant?" "The government shouldn't pay for their maternity leave too."

To put it simply, if you take a blanket generalization, apply it to a population of people, and say, "This is why we won't hire you. This could happen," well, that is technically discrimination.

❖❖❖❖❖❖❖❖❖❖❖❖❖❖❖❖❖❖❖❖❖❖❖❖❖❖❖❖❖❖❖

"I was staying the night in a separate bedroom. We were just friends and I trusted him. I'm not sure what he gave me during dinner, but I went into a deep sleep because of it. Next thing I know I'm waking up and he's climaxing in me. I shoved him off and cursed him out and left. He kept messaging and apologizing, and I kept ignoring him. I didn't think anyone would believe me if I reported it since I voluntarily spent the night. I knew they would side with him; he was well-liked. I got pregnant from the rape; it was the hardest decision of my life, but I kept the baby."

❖❖❖❖❖❖❖❖❖❖❖❖❖❖❖❖❖❖❖❖❖❖❖❖❖❖❖❖❖❖❖

I could open a business and say, "I won't hire any men because they are more likely to go to jail, statistically speaking." Legal? Yes. Ethical? Not really. Logical and sensible? No. Simply put, color, nationality, sex, and sexual orientation do not determine how valuable or not valuable of an asset someone will be to the military. Someone's capability for military service cannot truly be discovered until they are thrown in and put to the real test.

The military is, and might always be, the most discriminatory organization when it comes to hiring. It's unclear at times what's fair and what's not fair. To many, it makes sense that the military cannot have severely physically or mentally handicapped people enlisting. There have been people with diagnosed psychotic disorders who slip through the cracks and end up in a war zone unmedicated, and it's not a pretty outcome. A recruiter is asked to look for people with no mental health history, no medical issues (with some exceptions), no legal issues, no underage drinking, no illegal drug use, etc. In other words, recruiters are tasked with looking for a person who doesn't exist. I'm a freak of nature. I may have been the closest thing to that ideal list, and I still had a couple of spiked punch bowls back in my younger years.

The military is certainly making some progressive changes by including many populations of people who were denied the opportunity to serve despite being fully capable, able-bodied, and willing to serve. Recruiting people with willingness is extremely important, especially considering the U.S. military has had an all-volunteer force for decades. There is no single picture of what a service member looks like. Military members come in all shapes, sizes, sexes, nationalities, etc. It's truly incredible what can be accomplished when diverse people come together and let go of all their "isms."

PART III

PITFALLS

I'M NOT MYSELF ANYMORE

"The most important decision you will ever make is whether or not you will continue hating yourself."

Sometimes veterans survive military service and war but remain deeply disturbed by the things they did, the things they didn't do, or who they turned into. Moral injury is a big topic of discussion—and with good reason. Often, the military puts people in unique, stressful, off-the-wall situations that force them to react without an opportunity to think first. Sometimes it's a life-or-death situation. Sometimes it's a situation with orders that feel questionable, that don't sit well with one's inner conscience.

Enlisting in the military does not mean someone is prepared to be in life-or-death situations. It does not mean they know exactly what is coming their way or how they should react in a given scenario. All people really know is that they enlisted and can only hope it goes okay. Like most people, they try to make the best of it and train hard in hopes that the training will save them in the near future.

⬦⬦⬦⬦⬦⬦⬦⬦⬦⬦⬦⬦⬦⬦⬦⬦⬦⬦⬦⬦⬦⬦⬦⬦⬦⬦⬦⬦⬦⬦⬦⬦⬦⬦⬦⬦⬦⬦

"I was working at the child morgue for the past eight months while deployed. Every day we had to dispose of the dead bodies. Children that had been tortured, burned, broken bones.... I can't sleep anymore."

⬦⬦⬦⬦⬦⬦⬦⬦⬦⬦⬦⬦⬦⬦⬦⬦⬦⬦⬦⬦⬦⬦⬦⬦⬦⬦⬦⬦⬦⬦⬦⬦⬦⬦⬦⬦⬦⬦

Many veterans describe terrifying situations that leave them questioning whether they did the right thing, whether they are still worthy of happiness or life. And, all the while, they forget that they are a small and tiny portion of the population. They are being put through adverse combat experiences that the majority of people are never exposed to.

Regardless of how much training a troop receives—pre-exposure preparation" and combat training—they cannot predict outcome. Going into war is chaotic. No amount of money, time, or resources can ensure someone's safety. The chances of moral injury in the military are extremely high because there are lives at risk. Some will die, and some will go home. Trying to make sense of the outcome feels impossible, because war is often senseless. Even if it feels like the fight is for the right reasons or a cause bigger than oneself, people have a hard time making peace with someone else dying while they survived, or someone dying by their hands to ensure they survived.

Between survivor's guilt and various other types of moral injury, some veterans are inclined to punish themselves. Veterans may self-sabotage for the rest of their lives because of the chronic shame and guilt. It's not just about fearing for their lives. It's about learning to live with themselves after surviving and seeing the worst of the world. The traumatic memories keep gnawing on and deteriorating a troop's spirit.

Survival doesn't mean healing. Who are we after we have survived? Everyone who has been in a war zone or lived through another type of trauma needs to recognize that they are no longer who they were beforehand, and that's okay.

For example, now, I am Elisa, after Afghanistan. Who am I now? What happened? How did it impact me? How did I change? For both the good and the bad? What is my fault and what isn't my fault? Am I punishing myself for my mistakes, as well as the mistakes of others, far too much and too often?

Veterans must ask themselves these questions keeping in mind that we aren't meant to suffer from our mistakes...we are meant to learn from them.

"I'm not myself anymore" is one of the common lines I hear as a therapist. Not only can they often tell they aren't who they used to be, but they also have family members, friends, and spouses in their ears constantly reminding them that they have changed. Veterans often feel drastically different than everyone around them. Their moods are different than those of others on a daily basis. It goes beyond PTSD to include a daily internal struggle with a moral injury that has set in.

"Why can't I be happy like everyone else today?" "Why do I have a much shorter fuse?" "Why is putting up with bulls**t way harder than it used to be?" "Why don't I care anymore about the things everyone else cares about? About the things I used to care about?" "Everyone says I've changed."

❖◦❖◦❖◦❖◦❖◦❖◦❖◦❖◦❖◦❖◦❖◦❖◦❖◦❖◦❖◦❖◦❖◦❖◦❖

"My friend was standing right next to me when he was hit by a dud mortar. Although it did not explode, the blade of it sliced open his head in a slant. I could see his brains falling out as he hit the ground. I also saw how the blood soaked into the sand and made a clay-like substance. The sight of blood going into sand is a sight that stays with me for some reason."

❖◦❖◦❖◦❖◦❖◦❖◦❖◦❖◦❖◦❖◦❖◦❖◦❖◦❖◦❖◦❖◦❖◦❖◦❖

In Afghanistan, I was tasked to reschedule a client when his therapist went on a mission. The client looked sad, and I asked if he was okay or if he needed another therapist. He said no. I took his word for it despite the fact that his eyes looked troubled. Later that evening, that particular soldier shot himself with his M16 and died.

Every day since that moment, for what I presume will be the rest of my life, I blame myself. I noticed my blame wasn't just about ignoring my instincts as a mental health technician, but it was also about failing in my mission as a military member, which was even more devastating.

Veterans have to recognize that whatever is causing a deep moral injury isn't the only part of their story. Sometimes it cuts so deep that it is magnified until it becomes the only part of someone's identity, the only experiences they think about. Despite all the great things someone may have done, a moral injury can set them on the path of questioning everything about who they are, what their intentions were, and what they are worthy of.

I NEED MY MEDS

"The one thing that saved me and gave me hope for many years is also what's slowly destroying my body and mind, and now…I am forever torn."

Everyone chooses their poison(s). Not everyone is an addict, but everyone self-medicates. If people think they are alone in self-medicating, they thought wrong. Alternatively, some may just be thinking, "I've never done drugs! I don't self-medicate."

Self-medicating is what people do in order to feel better. That is all. It's that simple. Sometimes that involves people putting something into their bodies. Sometimes it's an act or behavior they engage in that releases endorphins. Most people are familiar with the extensive list of drugs, including alcohol and cigarettes. Whether something is legal is irrelevant when it comes to self-medicating.

Substance abuse is, of course, important and needs to be assessed, but what's not as common is posing questions about addictive or compulsive self-medicating behaviors such as: shopping, gambling, sex (sometimes including buying sex, porn, or strip clubs), video games, the internet, social media, TV, movies, etc. (Yes, I have heard it all.)

Many ask how people can tell when it becomes a problem, especially when it doesn't appear to be hurting someone as much as helping them cope with debilitating symptoms.

First, let's imagine a reasonably healthy person who isn't suffering from mental illness. What do they do to self-medicate? Perhaps on a bad day they eat some ice cream and drink a reasonably sized alcoholic beverage. Then, soon after, they're medicated and life goes on, still intact. They are even luckier if something healthy is more than enough to medicate them fully, such as exercise or reading.

Healthy people self-medicate from time to time when things get hard, but when they are back to equilibrium, they continue with life without any problem. However, mentally ill people who constantly suffer from anxiety, anger, depression, etc., on a daily basis are tempted to self-medicate a lot more. The more problems someone has, the more they are tempted to self-medicate. People tend to self-medicate with things that have made them feel good in the past, things that are proven to be effective in making them feel good. Or perhaps they self-medicate with things their friends have told them about.

Then, all of the sudden, what could have originally been a healthy or non-excessive way to self-medicate has -turned into a maladaptive habit that can cause long-lasting physical, financial, relational, and emotional damage. Excessive isn't a number I can assign. In the mental health and substance abuse world, there is never a one-size-fits-all.

❀❀❀❀❀❀❀❀❀❀❀❀❀❀❀❀❀❀❀❀❀❀❀❀❀❀❀❀❀

"A VBIED went off right next to me. My friend saved my life by making sure he did not get too close to my Humvee. I was a first responder after it went off. I tried to save my friend's life, but he died instantly. I went back to my unit with blood all over my uniform. My commander yelled at me for being there and trying to save people. He made me get back to work immediately. When I went in a different room to sit and decompress, he followed me in there and said: 'Maybe you weren't meant for war.' To this day, I still have my blood-soaked uniform. The blood of my friend. I can't let it go."

❀❀❀❀❀❀❀❀❀❀❀❀❀❀❀❀❀❀❀❀❀❀❀❀❀❀❀❀❀

To tell when a habit is good, bad, or becoming a substance abuse problem or addiction, listen to the people who love you. If they are all saying you have a problem, you just might. Listen to your bank account when it's suffering and screaming at you every month. You know what you're buying. Listen to your body and the excruciating health side effects.

Most importantly, I encourage my clients not to have shame. Everyone self-medicates almost every day. I did about five minutes ago!

o-⊕-o

"My last responsibility was to take care of Wounded Warriors. I spent my days seeing amputees and people that needed surgeries to be okay. Provide them with whatever they needed. A young girl soldier who had lost her leg cried while she talked about how her life would never be the same again. I was not mentally equipped for that type of day-to-day challenge. I did the best I could and went home and drank every day."

o-⊕-o

But, in all seriousness, while excessive self-medicating can become a big problem, shame is worse. Life is hard enough. Illness is hard enough. Do not hate yourself for having a perfectly human reaction to an imperfect life. When someone is sick, they take their medicine. And when someone is constantly sick, they might simply take too much if they lose touch with what is a "normal–sized" dose and when/if they are, in fact, medicated.

Most people with PTSD and other mental illnesses slip into a self-medicating-gone-wrong phase during their lives. The ones predisposed to developing addictions will be the really unlucky ones. If you can get treatment, I encourage you to get it right away—the sooner, the better.

Along with the urge to feel better, some veterans feel the need to have an adrenaline rush once again—a rush that almost feels like combat. Or maybe they just need to feel something, anything. Psychological numbing changes how one feels on a daily basis, and it's disturbing to not be able to connect with your emotions anymore. Self-medicating can become a way of connecting with those emotions again, even if it's not necessarily a healthy method.

If someone suffers from both a mental illness and a substance abuse issue, they're considered a "dual diagnosis" client. This doesn't mean the situation is hopeless; it means they need more treatment and they need to prioritize self-care. Everyone can heal and recover to some extent, but it's not going to be overnight. Therapists are looking for willingness more than anything else.

Many older clients express the fear that they are too old to change their habits, that they might just be too set in their ways. They are too used to the habits they developed, which are sometimes maladaptive habits and behaviors. But age has nothing to do with it. I've had teenaged clients who were next to impossible to work with because they were not voluntarily seeking treatment, while elderly clients sometimes make fast changes as their willingness has increased with self-insight. Therapists, along with a strong support network from the home environment, are able to help assist veterans with weaning off of substances—as long as there is willingness and persistence from the veteran too.

I MIGHT DO SOMETHING
I'LL REGRET

"A man will kill someone before he will ever speak his pain."

There was a soldier on my deployment who made fun of me every Thursday at karaoke night. Why? Because I was working in the combat stress clinic.

This soldier loved joking about mental health and how silly he felt it was. So the day he walked into the clinic with his face red, completely speechless, I knew something was up. I didn't make him stay in the waiting room with the others. I took him straight back to the assessment/triage office to see what was going on.

When the door closed and he had his privacy, he reported that he was very close to shooting his first sergeant in the face just a few hours ago in a meeting. He was full of rage. The combat stress team had to recommend his weapon get removed from him, for his safety and the safety of everyone around him.

Here's something I learned quickly in a combat zone: Troops in the combat zone are a lot more likely to have homicidal members—not just toward the enemy, but also toward each other.

Working on an Army forward operating base (FOB) I learned how common it is for service members to work together stateside, work together on deployment, and live together in very close quarters. They are stressed, angry, sleep-deprived, traumatized, and sick and tired of each other. Oh, and one other important thing: They are all armed!

⬦⬦⬦⬦⬦⬦⬦⬦⬦⬦⬦⬦⬦⬦⬦⬦⬦⬦⬦⬦⬦⬦⬦⬦⬦⬦⬦⬦⬦⬦⬦⬦⬦⬦⬦⬦⬦

"The enemies came right up near the wall in the VBIED, hit the sandbag barrier, and it exploded. They were trying to breach the base. I just used the gun and shot at them. I couldn't see. I couldn't hear. I just kept shooting and shooting, not knowing if I was hitting anything. I saw toward my right one of their suicide bombers. He climbed in between the sandbags. I shot at him. I'm not sure if the bomb he was wearing just went off or if I shot it and it went off, but I saw him explode quickly after."

⬦⬦⬦⬦⬦⬦⬦⬦⬦⬦⬦⬦⬦⬦⬦⬦⬦⬦⬦⬦⬦⬦⬦⬦⬦⬦⬦⬦⬦⬦⬦⬦⬦⬦⬦⬦⬦

Along with homicidal ideation, there are many other things that fall into the category of things veterans might regret. Things like walking off a FOB without permission and killing locals they are not authorized to kill. Or getting into a dramatic fistfight with a coworker or higher-up. Or keying your commander's car in a fit of rage.

PTSD is often associated with anger and rage. One of the biggest issues is that anger and rage are very easy to punish in the military. Leadership isn't interested in or educated about the root cause of rage. They are there to reinforce rules and regulations. They act on punishment very quickly, and the mental health factors often go unnoticed. They take corrective action for the problem, and they move on with the mission.

A very common theme I see in the clinical setting involves seeing veterans who have suffered in silence for so long that their lives deteriorated. Sometimes the rage simmers to the point where someone does something they regret, and now they're facing legal issues on top of everything else.

What may start as pure combat trauma can very easily manifest into PTSD with a substance abuse problem, then marital difficulties, work stress, financial issues, burnout, and, before they know it, they're getting into trouble. So many veterans with legal problems present with shock when they start treatment. They do not know how they got there. Where did it all go wrong? The amount of shame they feel is unspeakable, especially if they are coming for mandated mental health treatment. The powerlessness starts to set in when others are making decisions about their life and they have no control over the outcome.

✦✦✦✦✦✦✦✦✦✦✦✦✦✦✦✦✦✦✦✦✦✦✦✦✦✦✦✦✦✦✦✦✦✦✦✦

"It was supposedly just a rescue mission. We were supposed to just be in, save them, and get out. It was a riot though, and people weren't trying to let us through. The crowd attacked us and outnumbered us a great amount, to the point where we were ordered to attack them. We used our batons and pepper spray to attack the civilians. By the end of it all, most of them were on the ground suffering from baton injuries and crying heavily from the pepper spray being in their eyes, women and children too."

✦✦✦✦✦✦✦✦✦✦✦✦✦✦✦✦✦✦✦✦✦✦✦✦✦✦✦✦✦✦✦✦✦✦✦✦

Everyone who has gotten to the point where they fear they might do something they regret should have been in therapy years ago. Medical professionals always say preventative care is crucial for avoiding a medical crisis down the line, and it's the same when it comes to mental health. Starting therapy at the first warning signs could make all the difference in the world. Most veterans who commit these unspeakable, horrendous acts did not just snap one day. They did not get to that place overnight; they suffered for far too long without the help they needed.

Many people forget that underneath anger and rage lays pain and sadness. People get hurt before anger sets in. They express pain with anger if something is threatening their livelihood or emotional health. Many with "anger issues" often sum up their rage to randomness. It's not uncommon to hear, "I just go from calm to angry like that. I've always been that way and I cannot help it."

That line is a myth, but, unfortunately, anger management is not taught in an efficient or logical way. Discovering the root cause is imperative for healing—not just looking at what made a person explode right then and there, but also looking at the anger beneath the surface that has been waiting to come out for many years. The accumulated anger needs to be addressed.

◇◆◇◆◇◆◇◆◇◆◇◆◇◆◇◆◇◆◇◆◇◆◇◆◇◆◇◆◇◆◇◆◇◆◇◆◇◆◇

"An IED went off in the distance pretty close to us. We had to clean up the bones and body parts of the locals that died. Put them in plastic bags and tie them up. I also lost one of my friends out there. He was blown up by a VBIED off in the distance; we were ordered not to go and help since it would put our lives at risk too. I wanted to go and help."

◇◆◇◆◇◆◇◆◇◆◇◆◇◆◇◆◇◆◇◆◇◆◇◆◇◆◇◆◇◆◇◆◇◆◇◆◇◆◇

Many veterans remain in domestic situations or careers that continue to exacerbate their anger. They feel they are stuck and have no choice.

But there's almost always a choice. The outcomes are not always favorable but small changes need to be made and cemented on the daily.

My very first coach once told me, "You are not obligated to do anything from the moment you are born, except die." Meaning, most of what we believe are obligations are actually choices we are actively making, day in and day out.

Many veterans with suppressed, implosive, or explosive anger have a difficult time with accountability, especially because it's hard to place where their anger is coming from without therapy. I empower all of my clients to remember their freedom of will. If a person or situation has gotten them to the point of homicidal thoughts or impulsive decisions, it might be time to leave. Nothing is worth killing the emotional spirit and health, especially not things people will regret later.

I DON'T WANT TO LIVE ANYMORE

*"It could have killed me, and it would have been okay.
Because, in that moment, I lived for me. In that moment,
everything felt so right. In that moment, I felt a deep and
terrifying passion. There is no place I'd rather be…than
in that moment. So shoot me and kill me and let my last
memory be in that moment when I was happy."*

There is an infinite number of treatment modalities, coping
tools, self-soothing tactics, and self-care activities, but
without a will to live, nothing works. Without the will to live,
summoning up the energy to engage in anything that could
make you feel better might just feel next to impossible.

Severely traumatized people do not wake up with happiness. They must work hard for happiness, or even sometimes work hard just for contentment. They must put exhausting amounts of time and effort toward healing. Sometimes they want to give up. Why would anyone want to fight so hard for a life that feels depressing and empty? Why would anyone want to fight when they are around a lot of people who look like they would be so much happier and better off without them?

A rare number of people are actively suicidal, but a decent number of people have simply lost their will to live at least at some point in their lifetime. "I can see why so many veterans are killing themselves" is a common thing I hear, even from non-suicidal Veterans.

One of the most crucial parts of a suicidal assessment is the question: "Do you want to die? Or do you want to live with less pain?"

The many times I have posed this question, I have almost always gotten the answer back, "I want to live with less pain." Once I know they want to live with less pain, we must search for where their pain is coming from. How can we manage it? How can we establish the belief that the pain won't last forever, as well as the hope that there's something better after the pain is gone? It's a matter of teaching clients not to be hopeless, but to be hopeful. Dying might feel like a tempting thing when everything feels out of control, but everything won't be out of control forever. There is no permanent emotion or situation— but death is a permanent solution.

Maybe life has been rough for the past few years and someone is fed up and needs a safe outlet, like a therapist. In those cases, I let clients get it all out. I'm fine with screaming and cursing and bearing witness to the rage for what the military or others did to someone. That is what I'm there for. I don't expect happy people coming into my office. I know that if a client has shown up, they at least realized something was wrong. The harsh reality of pursuing happiness is that we must work extremely hard for it; it is not a natural or permanent state of being. Trauma makes it an even harder emotional state to pursue and cherish.

—

"There's one image that I can't let go of. It will always haunt me. I was walking into one of the hangers and saw two U.S. soldiers hanging by their necks, already dead. I'll never understand what possessed them to do that. Especially because of how young they both were."

—

The people who cannot fathom why someone would commit suicide are the people who have never wanted to die. Sometimes people even think that those who successfully commit suicide were too weak to handle war—or life in general.

But it's actually the exact opposite.

Most likely, those who successfully commit suicide have been through some of the worst experiences or some of the hardest emotional and mental symptoms, all while working hard at their jobs and raising families. We, as a society, do not understand suicidal ideation, gestures, attempts, plans, intent, etc. The DOD has its annual suicide awareness and prevention training in the form of what we have coined "death by PowerPoint" presentations.

◊-◊

"One guy got a Dear John letter not too long before we went under attack again. He was so depressed and suicidal he said he was going to walk into the incoming fire. He got up and started moving quickly toward it. I had to fight him and tackle him to the ground just to save his life at that point."

◊-◊

The longer I work in the mental health profession, the more I hate those presentations. There is a large focus on warning signs and what the lower-ranking troops need to do to help their battle buddy not want to kill themself. Meanwhile, the higher ranks put ongoing pressure on lower ranks to perform more often and better than before.

If a troop asks for a "mental health day," there's a good chance someone is laughing in their face or just telling them "no." In the military, they are now trying to preach mental health care, resiliency, and looking after fellow battle buddies, but very few are taking the actions necessary to ensure people are actually mentally stable. It's not a part of "the mission;" therefore, it's not their responsibility. If command is concerned that a troop is at risk, they can put the troop in for a command-directed evaluation with mental health on the basis of their suspicions. Military members have fewer rights than civilians, and they can be mandated to go to mental health in some cases. Unfortunately, those recommendations are typically due to behavioral concerns or issues with how the troop's mental health is interfering with the mission. An exact mandated reporting measure for military mental health is termed "endangerment to the mission."

It's a lot to ask of lower-ranking enlisted. They are asked to do their job and also somehow prevent their coworker's suicide before it happens. Also, leadership may have zero clue what the state of the morale in their unit is. They may not be physically or mentally present enough to see a hostile work environment. So, the increased attention on mental health is focused on protecting the mission more than ensuring overall mental health preventatively.

There are a high number of people—both in the military and post-war veterans—who need help and are not getting treatment. Many people ask what's wrong with the mental health system. They ask why the mental health system can't save them all. But they often forget that a big part of the issue is the lack of mental health treatment altogether: the stigma, avoidance, not enough staff, veterans being put on long, VA waiting lists before they even get a psych visit, bad treatment, or treatment not tailored for them.

The bottom line is: Suicide is hard to predict, even for the professionals. We will always be taught statistics about who is more likely to commit suicide and why. We are given many statistics every year to remind us that suicide rates are still high. We know this already, but knowledge doesn't always mean proper action is being taken. Also, despite the learning materials and lectures, and safety planning by therapists, not everyone gives off warning signs, not everyone gets saved.

There is one major thing we do have control over, and that is how we treat each other in the work environment. The military cannot always control who someone dates, how they spend their money, or whether or not they have a mental illness. What they can do is make sure they come to a healthy work environment. A work environment that is so trustworthy that a troop feels comfortable asking to go to mental health if needed. If the DOD puts as much focus on creating that type of work environment as they have on "death by PowerPoint," they just might get somewhere.

PART IV

FORWARD

EVERY STORY IS UNIQUE

"Most people do not possess the capability of listening with unconditional acceptance."

We should never be under the impression that we know someone's story just because we know their military branch, job in the military, rank, sex, gender, or the war they fought in. With as many stories as I've heard in my career, I can attest to the fact that each one is unique.

One of the most common questions I get from other clinicians and mental health students is: "What intervention do you give your veteran clients?"

I hate this question.

I take each individual client, conduct a full assessment, and tailor a treatment plan accordingly. Not the other way around. I don't have a secret divine intervention. No "one-size-fits-all." No one thing works for everyone.

Even the so-called evidenced-based treatments that are all the rave and are said to "cure PTSD" aren't one-size-fits-all miracle treatments. I've had many clients who received prolonged exposure treatment, cognitive processing therapy, and EMDR. But some of them are still suffering from PTSD years later, even after being marked as "in remission" by some of their previous therapists. Why? Because the moment veterans feel they are "better," they typically stop all therapy and move on with life in hopes that everything will be "normal" from then on out. Unfortunately, veterans are still human, and humans get triggered or retraumatized and symptoms can come back in a flurry. It's important to note that if a client does not fit into the "mold" and respond well to a treatment modality, they must be accommodated with something else, and they should not be looked at as a lost cause.

⬦⬦⬦⬦⬦⬦⬦⬦⬦⬦⬦⬦⬦⬦⬦⬦⬦⬦⬦⬦⬦⬦⬦⬦⬦⬦⬦⬦⬦⬦⬦⬦⬦⬦⬦

"I was sitting casually and all of a sudden I see four mortars flying right above my head. I see someone running the wrong direction, right into the danger zone. I got up and had to tackle him to make sure he didn't end up dead."

⬦⬦⬦⬦⬦⬦⬦⬦⬦⬦⬦⬦⬦⬦⬦⬦⬦⬦⬦⬦⬦⬦⬦⬦⬦⬦⬦⬦⬦⬦⬦⬦⬦⬦⬦

We have to be careful about our assumptions of what works as far as treatment and what stories and traumas we perceive veterans to have. Some veterans say war wasn't even the hardest part of their story. It may have been the people they worked with. Maybe someone's trauma wasn't combat trauma at all, but military sexual trauma. Just because someone is a woman veteran doesn't mean she was assaulted, and just because someone is a male veteran doesn't mean he wasn't assaulted. Someone who deployed didn't necessarily deploy to a battlefield. Perhaps it was a ship or a submarine. Perhaps they have secondary trauma and compassion fatigue due to drone operations. Some people say they loved the military but hated their job. Some loved their job but hated the military or the rigid structure of the organization. Some veterans are simply bored out of their minds and miss home. And then, some people are actually okay after they serve and do not want to be viewed as "broken" or "ill."

Those who interact with veterans need to listen more. We need to hear their stories. We need to be aware of our own bias, stigmas, and lack of education. I, like many veterans, have gotten let's say interesting comments and assumptions over the years regarding my service. If you ask veterans sincere questions about what they did and how their career was, you often get sincere answers. It's much better to genuinely ask than to guess and assume.

Look at it this way. If someone works for the airport, we don't just assume they are a pilot. They could be a TSA agent, or maybe they work in one of the restaurants. Maybe they are a flight attendant or the person who checks the bags. It's the same concept for the military. Some military members are infantry with a higher chance that they will engage in war conflict on the ground, while some are pilots engaging in air combat. In my case, I worked in a mental health clinic as part of a medical group that included medics, pharmacy techs, dentists, etc. There are cooks and people who work in finance, or people who work on the vehicle engines or aircraft or ship maintenance. There are firefighters and military police. There are military members in various types of special forces operations with top secret clearances, which also means there are a lot of government secrets they cannot divulge, not even in therapy sessions.

In other words, when someone says they were in the military, it doesn't provide much information at all. It paints a picture that is perhaps inaccurate. Follow-up questions are necessary to grasp what someone did in the military and what they sacrificed when they served.

◦◦◦◦◦◦◦◦◦◦◦◦◦◦◦◦◦◦◦◦◦◦◦◦◦◦◦◦◦◦◦◦◦◦◦◦◦

"I stood up too high and the mortar hit beside me and shrapnel hit both of my legs and I was almost left for dead. My team panicked and started to run away because we were being surrounded. The enemy was getting closer and closer. I couldn't move. I could only raise my hand and hope that someone stopped for me. Finally my friend had to make a difficult choice and he ran and came back for me and dragged me out of there. After my medevac they had me getting medical care for a couple months, only to send me right back in. I did everything I could to avoid all missions. Death felt more real for me then. After having that near-death experience, I knew I wasn't invincible anymore. The friend that saved me ended up taking my place in a mission, along with other guys in my platoon. Their helicopter got shot down and they all died."

❖◦

There was a sociology professor teaching on my base my first semester of college. She had never been exposed to the military in any capacity. At the beginning of one of our classes, she said, "Man the guy at the gate checked my ID. I feel sorry for you guys having to stand at the gate like that all the time!"

We had to explain to her that not all military members do that. Only security forces (Air Force military police) have that responsibility. She was shocked to learn the military has its own cops. She then proceeded to ask, "Wait, so, you guys all have different jobs?"

We all took the time to explain our jobs and educate her. She even went so far as to say, "Well, I have no clue what you guys do. I thought maybe y'all marched around and stuff."

In addition, she often freaked out when she saw our glazed eyes staring at her monotonous PowerPoints. She was so used to civilian students half passed out at their desks. As military members, we sat up and listened with discipline, even when we weren't really "present." She sometimes let us leave early when she couldn't handle our stares as we faked paying attention like we were in a commander's call.

Comments and perceptions like that professor's can infuriate some veterans. I always try to take the path of educating misinformed civilians. The more I educate them, the less likely they are to offend veterans and military members in the future, which is safer for everyone. A powerful step for veterans adjusting to life post-service is being accepted by their civilian counterparts. There can be a mutual trust and respect if effort is made by both parties to hear each person's unique story.

IT'S NOT WEAKNESS

"Say the words that have been left unsaid, and shed the tears that you have not yet shed, and always know that your feelings are never wrong."

What is so wrong about feeling sad about the bad things that have happened to us? Why is sadness or grief so wrong? Why is crying so wrong? What is the purpose of a feeling? The purpose of a feeling is to tell us something. It sends us messages that are important for us to process and understand.

We can argue judgments and opinions all day, but we cannot argue feelings. A person feels what they feel, and sometimes it goes beyond all rationale. I tell clients all the time that they have a right to their feelings, and no one can argue otherwise.

Emotions are never wrong.

Emotions often get shamed, minimized, or distracted from. It is part of my job to help veterans come back to their feelings and process them. More often than not, people are made to feel like they shouldn't be upset or sad. So people get upset, and then upset at themselves for being upset. It's a vicious cycle. People are often alone in this sadness and shame, and if they speak up, they fear the worst: that their feelings will get invalidated once again.

❖❖❖❖❖❖❖❖❖❖❖❖❖❖❖❖❖❖❖❖❖❖❖❖❖❖❖❖❖❖❖❖❖

"I was a reporter in a combat zone. I saw everything and filmed as much as I possibly could with a camera on my shoulder and a rifle slung around me. I recorded raids, people dying from gunshots and explosions. One of the more aggravating things is how much the media lied about what was really going on, and how much I had to filter what I recorded."

❖❖❖❖❖❖❖❖❖❖❖❖❖❖❖❖❖❖❖❖❖❖❖❖❖❖❖❖❖❖❖❖❖

It is emotionally hazardous for veterans to suffer alone in their embarrassment about their feelings, especially if they already hate themselves for something as basic as being human. For to not have emotions at all implies that you are very unhealthy. Having emotions, including the embarrassing ones, implies you are a healthy, normal human being.

Most humans do not understand the purpose of emotion. Sadness is not inherently evil; it tells you that you are not happy with what is going on. Anxiety reminds you of your lack of control or feelings of powerlessness in what may be a too intense situation for you at the time. Anger may be telling you that something or someone is a threat to your peace. Guilt can remind you to be a more humble, better version of yourself. If we treated emotions the same way we treat a physical injury, we would interpret the internal pain and go about fixing the problem. Unfortunately, unhealthy cognitions and behaviors, as well as potentially toxic people in society, tend to interfere with the process of interpreting and processing emotions in a healthy manner. "I should have done…" "I shouldn't have felt…" "I'm horrible for…" "I don't want to feel anxious or depressed, so I'll just…"

Fighting emotions is one of the unhealthiest things a human being can do, and military members are literally trained to do just that. I have to put this in perspective for veterans all the time. Somewhere along the line, veterans are made to think they cannot—or should not—feel. They are forced into believing that feeling is a weakness that hinders the mission and will cause embarrassment to themselves and their unit.

But feelings are not weakness.

Feelings are just feelings.

Despite someone's service or military rank, they are still human. I know. I've seen colonels cry too.

✧◦

"There were children all over our vehicles begging for food and making it impossible to drive through. We were ordered to make our way through, and I know that we had to have run over some of them in the process."

❖◦❖◦❖◦❖◦❖◦❖◦❖◦❖◦❖◦❖◦❖◦❖◦❖◦❖◦❖◦❖◦❖◦❖◦❖◦

That being said, I hope to remove the stigma around getting mental health counseling as much as I can, knowing it will not go away completely. For veterans' sakes, I try to reinforce that they are no longer in the DOD; therefore, the risk of receiving therapy is much lower. I also tell them to keep in mind that anyone can go to therapy voluntarily and then from there decide if they like it, love it, or hate it.

If someone hates their therapist, they can switch therapists. If someone hates therapy altogether, they can just stop going. If someone is adamant about never putting psychotropic meds in their body, they can deny meds. Sometimes people fear mental health because they forget that they still have freedom of will regardless of what a therapist or doctor recommends.

Therapy is also still—and always will be—confidential, keeping in mind that mandated reporting is specifically for risk of harm to self, others, or children.

For those still in the military, it's hard to say whether going to therapy will impact their job or enlistment. I've seen some who have had to switch military career fields due to their mental illness. I've seen some get med boarded out due to their mental illness. But I've also seen some go to counseling regularly and go on to have a wonderful military career.

It is anxiety provoking and extremely difficult for a veteran to allow themselves that type of vulnerability. It means telling a complete stranger many things about themselves that they have tried so long and hard to hide. It's a risk, but there are many rewards if someone can open their mind to it, especially if they find the right therapist. Although, I'll admit, even I didn't enter therapy until I was twenty-seven. I was just as stubborn as everyone else, and before I entered therapy, I was in denial and military mode.

◦-◦

"We had taken in enemy hostages. All we had to do was watch them, but some of the guys decided to hurt and torture them instead. I wanted to say something or stop it, but nothing came out of my mouth."

◦-◦

Voluntarily going to therapy is simply requesting the help of a trained, neutral third party so that you don't have to handle all of your internal and overwhelming emotions alone. Two perspectives are usually better than one. To put it in a non-stigmatized perspective, I'll quote what my favorite psychiatrist kept repeating over and over again: "The brain is an organ." All organs and body parts should get treatment when there's a problem—nothing more and nothing less. Getting treatment is not a weakness; it's a response that can help sort out the distressing symptoms that might come with human emotion post-trauma.

HOW TO THERAPIST
AND HOW TO CLIENT

"All it may take is one harsh reaction or quick judgment, and they may never want to open up to you again."

There is no perfect therapist, no perfect client, but there is a way we can learn these roles and do our best to make the relationship as positive and effective as possible. Building rapport within the therapeutic relationship is crucial. No doubt you or someone you know has had negative experiences in therapy, so let's take a deeper look.

As a client, your role is to gain insight into your condition, have a healthy level of open-mindedness, and have a willingness to improve yourself and hold yourself accountable for your life, self-care, and well-being. A therapist is a helpful, empathetic, trained third party. They are meant to help, but you must help yourself first. Sometimes therapists offer supportive confrontations; they may challenge or push you. Sometimes it gets uncomfortable, and it never works as fast as we would like it to. Expectation management and respect for the therapeutic process is key.

With that being said, clients have rights. Social work and mental health work are about empowerment. The illness doesn't define someone; instead, people define how they will overcome it. It's about learning your limitations and how to work with those limitations so that you can still have a healthy and fulfilling life. If your intuition tells you otherwise during sessions, you can always request another therapist or find another clinic. That is your right.

There is typically only one hour a week for a therapy session, leaving clients with 167 hours on their own. However, that one therapy hour isn't the only time that should be spent on healing, self-care, and mental health. Mental well-being deserves much more time and attention than that. It is up to the client to take the tools they learn from therapy and implement them into daily life. Take what works, discard the rest, wash, rinse, and repeat.

The role of the therapist is to provide an in-depth assessment and develop a treatment plan to care for the needs and wants of the client. Patience and unconditional acceptance are some of a therapist's greatest virtues. Humans do not change quickly. Humans don't necessarily learn quickly. Humans might resist when new solutions are presented. They might self-sabotage and destroy their progress. They might not want for themselves what you want for them. So, therapists must have patience with this process; there is much that a therapist should not take personally.

◊◈◊◈◊◈◊◈◊◈◊◈◊◈◊◈◊◈◊◈◊◈◊◈◊◈◊◈◊◈◊◈◊◈◊

"I was a part of a quick reaction force team. I saw five men running out of a tank on fire, and there was nothing at that point we could do to save them. I'll never forget the smell of burning flesh."

◊◈◊◈◊◈◊◈◊◈◊◈◊◈◊◈◊◈◊◈◊◈◊◈◊◈◊◈◊◈◊◈◊◈◊

Much of the client-therapist relationship has to do with trust. When in doubt, establish trust. Know that sometimes there isn't a solution for someone's pain, and sometimes therapists are there to sit with someone for a while in a miserable situation they cannot escape just yet (especially if you work with military members still under contract!). Know that many veterans have a lot to process from their past but may not be willing to confront those things just yet. Know that some clients have immediate needs but might only want to dwell and ruminate on the past. It all goes back to meeting the client where they are.

Despite what some therapists say, if a client wants to talk about something, it's worth talking about. If they are still "living in the past," then the past truly impacted them that deeply. The emotions are still there and must be processed. If a client is ignoring emotions and crucial traumas that should be addressed, they're not ready. Always re-engage and remind them why they came to therapy, but never push them before they are ready.

I am not the best therapist. I have some clients who would probably rather have another therapist but are too afraid to say it. I also have some clients who have expressed that I am their favorite. When describing why, these clients often report that I treat them like a human. Veterans face many government gatekeepers from the time they enlist, throughout their service, and even post-service when applying for any type of benefit or resource. It's an endless series of people talking in circles with fake smiles on their faces paired with constant rejection. Therefore, I refuse to come off as another "government gatekeeper."

"Don't ask me if I killed anyone, the things I did...the things that we had to do out there, it was to survive, that's it. That's all I will say on that topic. It took me twenty-three years...twenty-three years to even speak on a single thing that happened in that war."

We cannot tell the traumatized to become more rational. They were traumatized; therefore, they get triggered. We cannot tell them to let go of their military identities; their military career was a huge part of their lives and makes up a significant portion of who they are today. We cannot tell them to let the rage and pain go when it has impacted them so deeply and usually still impacts them on a daily basis. We cannot pretend we have a simple solution when there is a complex series of grief, traumas, stressors, adjustment, and identity issues. Despite popular misconceptions, trauma and grief have no timelines. Veterans are living in the mind of a person who has been conditioned for and subjected to war. There is no erasing those experiences or rushing the art of healing.

This may not be 'evidence based,' but it is both a personal and professional account of what it means to be a veteran with PTSD. How trauma has a way of intricately and sneakily seeping into every aspect of a person's being. And how the very nature of being a military member means rejecting all emotion and making the ultimate sacrifice: self-sacrifice. It means no longer allowing pain to be an option, because they are never allowed to quit. Although the pain is very real, it often lurks in the shadows, unseen.

FAQS:
MYTHS DEBUNKED

This is a list of questions or comments I've received from the civilian population, and even some veterans. I've included answers in order to debunk myths and educate to the best of my ability.

Q: "Why are Veterans homeless? Why is that an issue? Don't they get paid for the rest of their lives?"

A: To answer this one, I have to first explain what a veteran is. In many cases, a veteran is considered to be someone who has served for at least 36 active duty months and/or deployed to a foreign war. However, someone cannot retire from the military or collect a pension unless they serve 20 years or more. Also, you must have received an honorable discharge to get the full benefits initially listed in your military contract. If a veteran does not get discharged honorably, they must go through an extensive legal process in hopes of a discharge upgrade, and that is not a guarantee. There are many veterans who haven't retired but you may notice they collect a disability payment every month. That isn't a pension. To get disability, they must go through a very hefty legal process and prove to a panel that the military damaged them enough mentally and/or physically that they deserve to be compensated for it both monetarily and with medical and mental health treatment. The average wait time to complete this process is typically 6–12 months. Many veterans do not get paid for the rest of their lives after service and there are many factors leading to the issue of veteran homelessness. Sometimes they get pushed out of the military before they anticipated. Sometimes they develop substance abuse issues. In fact, combat veterans are more likely to abuse alcohol than anyone else in the country. Sometimes their physical and mental injuries hinder their ability to complete a degree and their college GI bill depletes. Sometimes they are too mentally or physically damaged to keep gainful employment.

Q: "Why can't they just get over the war and trauma? It happened years ago!"

A: The hippocampus and the amygdala (parts of the brain) have a relationship to PTSD symptoms. Research what a trauma trigger is and how debilitating it can be on both mental and physical health. When the trauma happened, is only one factor to the equation. Did they get therapy early on? Are there other pre-existing mental health conditions? Did they have a good support system? What's the living environment and community like? For example, if someone goes from having a combat trauma to living in a domestic violence situation, are they able to heal? No, they aren't safe yet, so healing hasn't even started. Keep in mind that many veterans strive to get over trauma and war. They go through intense measures to avoid triggers and feelings. The suffering isn't a choice but is often linked to triggers that they have not identified or learned to manage just yet.

Q: "How can a grown man that size get raped?"

A: This question was posed to me by someone who was assuming rape is only a one-on-one situation. I explained that perhaps that person was gang raped or had a gun to his head. Another possibility is that he was drugged and raped in his sleep. Yes, this stuff happens on base sometimes too. Maybe the person who assaulted him was stronger and overpowered him. Anyone can be raped: male, female, strong, or not strong. Perpetrators are looking to find people when they are in vulnerable states and unaware of the danger that's lurking.

Q: "Is secondary trauma real?"

A: Secondary trauma is witnessing others suffer or hearing trauma stories. There are certain career fields that are at high risk: medics, nurses, doctors, therapists, lawyers, firefighters, cops, etc. Hearing trauma stories or constantly seeing people suffer shapes our views of the world around us. Gaining repeated knowledge of bad things happening in the world heightens anxiety and depression while diminishing one's sense of safety. With enough repetition and time, a person can start to suffer from PTSD symptoms through the trauma they see or hear others suffer from. It is chronic and complex. When in these career fields, it's extra important to engage in self-monitoring and self-care. It's also important for everyone to monitor their own exposure to trauma stories. Now that virtually everyone has access to horrific stories going on in their community and around the world via constant online exposure, technically anyone can be at risk of a buildup of secondary traumas.

Q: "Going into the military is for people that aren't educated and can't get into college."

A: There are many ways to define what it means to learn and get educated. The military is a different style of learning than going to a college. I'm not here to give my opinion on which education is better. Truthfully, it's just different. The military starts with technical training right after boot camp. Tech school is wedged between boot camp and the first permanent duty station. It's full-time learning, over forty hours a week of formal education about their soon-to-be military job. The schooling ranges from five weeks to twelve months. My mental health technical training was roughly three and a half months back in 2008. After tech school, we are immersed into doing our jobs, on-the-job training every single day. Depending on your unit, you may be encouraged, pressured, or mandated to start going to college part-time. Many military supervisors now see it as promoting growth for a new troop. Some branches require an associate degree at minimum for their enlisted members by the time they get up to higher NCO (noncommissioned officer) tier. When veteran status is achieved honorably, Veterans are then awarded their college GI bill. After the enlistments are up, many veterans use their college benefits to enhance their professional development. So, yes, they are capable of getting into college and earning a degree both while serving and post-service. It happens every year. Military members are getting a good amount of education. The style and order of events is what differs from the typical civilian path.

Q: "Everyone that served in the military has PTSD."

A: PTSD is a mental health condition that may come on after an acute trauma event or repeated chronic trauma exposure. Not everyone who serves in the military is exposed to trauma. Also, there are some who, despite being exposed to trauma, do not develop the condition. There are many factors involved, to include: biological susceptibility, support system or lack thereof, insight, motivation to receive help, as well as the level of the trauma one is exposed to. There is a stigma around "the angry combat vet with PTSD." This stigma is used as a scare tactic, a way to win a case in a legal argument against veterans. Or maybe an excuse for a toxic family member who does not want to take any responsibility for domestic issues. It can also be used by an angry employer or disgruntled employees who serve veterans but don't really want to serve them. Not all veterans will develop PTSD, and the veterans who do suffer from PTSD aren't necessarily going to blow up and attack people.

Q: "People with PTSD are crazy."

A: PTSD is not a psychotic disorder. A couple of examples of disorders in the psychotic realm include schizophrenia and delusional disorder. PTSD, which was formerly on the anxiety spectrum, is now in the category labeled "trauma and stressor related disorders." It is also accompanied by acute stress disorder and adjustment disorders. Many describe themselves as feeling "crazy" after they have dealt with PTSD symptoms. Many others look at people with PTSD as crazy. Crazy is not an official mental illness or symptom of any kind. It's a word used loosely due to the social stigma of mental illness. Post-traumatic stress disorder is exactly that: high stressors, triggers, and symptoms following trauma(s).

Q: "Is enlisting worth it? Should I join? A lot of people tell me 'Don't do it!' Is it really that bad?"

A: This is not a yes or no answer. There is no way I can look into the future and be able to tell if your hypothetical future military career would be worth it or not. Some describe the military as the best decision they ever made. Others report major regret about joining and feel it was not worth the pain and suffering it caused. Following their question is usually a series of responses they have already gotten from friends and family members, some of whom never served and only know things based on hearsay. I tell everyone the same answer when they ask me this question: "Do not let anyone talk you into joining, but do not let anyone talk you out of it either. It truly has to be your decision, for it is an all-volunteer force, and you need to decide for yourself if you believe it will be worth the sacrifice."

SELF-INTERVENTIONS

Below are some symptoms that are common when suffering from PTSD paired with the many ways veteran clients have reported being able to cope, self-sooth, or lower the intensity of a particular symptom. This is by no means a replacement for therapy. Please, if you are suffering, go to therapy. As a means of self-help, I wanted to share this list. Remember that what works for one person may not work for another. Listen to your mind and body as you experiment with various coping strategies.

Depression: Exercise, funny movies, traveling, setting goals and taking action toward objectives, reading, writing, socializing, cooking, art therapy, avoid redundancies and shake up the routine every now and then. When symptoms are severe, engage in self-care and enjoy your solitude activities as well as time with others. Find your balance.

Hypervigilance/anxiety: Soothing bubble baths, chew on ice, engage logical portion of the brain (math problems, shapes, colors, critical thinking), deep breathing, guided imagery, yoga, progressive muscular relaxation, music, be aware of and write down your triggers. Track and confront any irrational thinking patterns or themes that may exist, leave triggering situations when possible and appropriate.

Sleep deprivation: Phone on silent and never on the bed or under your pillow, no stimulating activities right before bed, use bed for sex and sleep only, consistent bedtime routine, service dogs, schedule a sleep study, melatonin, find the environment you're most relaxed and comfortable in (e.g., dark and no noise versus background noise and dim lights).

Irritability/rage: Walk away from trigger if possible, practice assertiveness versus aggression, critically evaluate people in your life and stay away from toxicity, martial arts, talk therapy. If there's built-up rage, an outlet is very crucial. Find calming objects and/or objects you can fidget with.

Intrusive thoughts: Process emotions and memories versus suppressing or pushing them away, enjoyable activity in solitude versus isolation without plans, meditation, journaling, talking with a trusted friend, let yourself cry if you need to. Do not reject or feel shame in feeling or remembering the hardships.

Isolation: Socialize in small spurts in less triggering environments, invite friends and family over, be selective about your go-to places, but make sure you are still going out and learning to trust some of your surroundings once again. Fun in solitude is good, but isolating constantly due to fear of triggers can be maladaptive and mentally harmful.

Honorable mentions: These are activities that have been reported as extremely helpful for PTSD and address multiple symptoms:

- Brazilian Jiu Jitsu (amazing camaraderie)
- Cannabis (indica strain for anxiety/ hypervigilance, sativa strain for depressive symptoms, hybrid strain if you suffer from both anxiety and depression)
- Group therapy (very helpful for the peer-to-peer support and the knowledge you are not alone in suffering)
- Nature! As cheesy as it sounds, be one with nature as much as possible: forests, beaches, mountains, etc. Natural healing agents!

Things to avoid as much as possible:

- **Alcohol:** Although a very powerful temporary potion to address anxiety, it's highly addictive and associated with some of the deadliest withdrawal symptoms known to man. Keep it at a minimum, as well as other hard drugs. Also be cautious with prescription meds and take them only as prescribed by a doctor. They might be prescribed, but it is possible to abuse prescription drugs as well.
- **Constant Isolation:** Although tempting to avoid triggers, we need human contact. Also, in order to accomplish goals, we inevitably need to go out into the world. Too much isolation can lead to full-blown

agoraphobia, which can hinder short- and long-term life goals.

- **Toxic relationships:** The first step of treating PTSD is establishing safety. If someone's living environment involves domestic violence or emotional and/or physical abuse, it will heavily trigger their trauma symptoms. Veterans in toxic relationships often have a pattern of taking one step forward and two steps back. Harmful relationships are often described as a battlefield for a reason.

ADDITIONAL RESOURCES

It's important to remember that if you want to apply for any benefit, seek the expert! If you want to use your college GI bill, find a GI bill specialist. If you need help with housing, find a housing specialist with your local VA or a nonprofit nearby. If you want to make a claim, go through the veteran benefits administration or find a veteran service officer (VSO).

Do not, I repeat, do not take someone's word for it. Don't even take my word for it! Although many of your veteran buddies may have applied for benefits and given you sound advice, they are not the experts, and their story is different than yours. They may be eligible for something you aren't eligible for. They might be in a different state that has more funding for veterans.

Also, keep in mind that everything changes. As of now you might be eligible for something, and then next year you aren't. Programs lose funding, forms change, processes change, the workers change, information gets lost, etc.

With that being said, I'm concluding this book with a list of resources you or your veteran family member may want to look into. This list doesn't guarantee you get it. It's just a list of what I'm aware of. There is a lot more available for veterans than this list: things I may not know about yet, cities and states I've never lived in before may have more resources or may not have a resource I'm listing. So, one more time, always consult the professionals. Never assume you're eligible until you do an intake for a program.

The veteran benefits administration, as well as the veteran hospital administration, is very complex. You will never run into any VA employee who can give you all the answers to the questions you have. Everyone has a specialty and, no matter how educated anyone is, it is impossible for anyone to know all things regarding veteran benefits and veteran hospital services. Also, getting help from any VA agency will feel a lot different than when you (a veteran) got help in the DOD. The speed, efficiency, and customer service is drastically different! Manage your expectations accordingly.

Mental Health
- VA medical center mental health clinic
- VA medical center substance abuse clinic
- Vet centers: they offer readjustment counseling for combat veterans and military sexual trauma

- Check if there are any local nonprofits in your city that offer free counseling for veterans and family members.

Housing

- HudVash for veterans in the shelter who are registered as homeless. You may qualify for voucher and low rent.
- SSVF (supportive services for veteran families) Grants for low-income veterans at risk of homelessness (usually meaning an eviction notice or already homeless); you could potentially qualify for support for moving and a grant.
- If you are homeless, inform the shelter you are enrolling in that you are a veteran; they may be able to accommodate with a veteran-only shelter.

Employment

- Vocational Rehabilitation (Voc Rehab) is an employment program that helps provide job training and job accommodations for veterans with disability (as of now, those who are 20 percent disabled or higher can apply for the program)
- Search for nonprofits in your local area that help provide veterans with employment
- If you are enrolled in college with GI bill or Voc Rehab, inquire about the VA work/study program. (If you qualify, you get paid a stipend to work at a nearby VA facility tailored to fit your school schedule.)

File for Disability

Note: Veterans file for disability typically after military enlistment. If there is any physical or mental condition you suffer from that either onset or was exacerbated by military service, you are entitled to file a claim for disability compensation. Compensation is awarded based off of the decision of the VBA—not the hospital! It's a long legal process. Proof is a big determinant but it's not always a deal breaker if you do not have proof (especially when it comes to mental health as many veterans avoided treatment while they were in the military).

To file a claim visit:

- Your local veteran benefits administration office
- Service officers at VAMCs or the state department of veteran affairs offices
- American Legions/VFWs/DAVs
- Online: Ebenefits.va.gov

Financial

- Check for veteran scholarships or local nonprofits that help provide relief or aid to veterans
- Check for free financial coaching in your area
- Go to your local financial aid or social welfare office. Inquire about SNAP or financial aid and inform them of your veteran status

Medical

- Enroll in your local VA; call and request enrollment forms from an outreach manager or fill out enrollment forms online
- If you are a disabled OIF, OEF veteran, look into the VA caregiver program (stipend for spouse/family member who is a caregiver to a veteran)

Spiritual

- VA chaplains
- Check your local area for programs that provide free spiritual/social retreats for veterans

Legal

- Look into local nonprofits that assist in discharge upgrade or DD214 amendments if needed
- For substance abuse related legal issues, search for a veterans treatment court

Burial benefits

Find your local national cemetery for veterans. If you register before death, it saves your family a lot of work. Many burials for honorably discharged veterans come at little to no charge as long as they are buried in the national cemetery under Veterans Affairs funding or Arlington National Cemetery for the Army.

❀❀❀❀❀❀❀❀❀❀❀❀❀❀❀❀❀❀❀❀❀❀❀❀❀❀❀❀❀

Have your DD214 on hand always! It is what I have coined as the "golden ticket" to getting almost all veteran resources after your discharge from the U.S. military.

❀❀❀❀❀❀❀❀❀❀❀❀❀❀❀❀❀❀❀❀❀❀❀❀❀❀❀❀❀

ABOUT THE AUTHOR

Elisa Escalante grew up in Texas and California throughout most of her childhood. Twelve days after her high school graduation in June of 2008, she enlisted in the United States Air Force and was selected to be a mental health technician. Elisa served six years active duty on Dyess Air Force base Texas, working in the mental health clinic at the medical group, serving Air Force troops and their dependents with mental health needs. In 2012, she deployed to Afghanistan to work at the combat stress clinic and support deployed soldiers on a forward operating base. After her active duty career ended in 2014, Elisa moved to New York City after being accepted to NYU Silver School of Social Work. During her studies, she also served as a Mental Health Noncommissioned officer in the Air Force reserves at Westover Air Reserve base, Massachusetts.

Elisa became a licensed Master of Social Work (LMSW) in July 2017, and in September of 2017, began her first and current civilian career providing counseling services to combat veterans and veterans who suffered from military sexual trauma. Elisa completed 10 years total of Air force service in the summer of 2018 and separated honorably. In June of 2020, Elisa earned an advanced certification in veteran services and is estimated to test for her advanced clinical license (LCSW) in 2021.

CPSIA information can be obtained
at www.ICGtesting.com
Printed in the USA
JSHW032336150621
15923JS00003B/192